Financing Foreign Trade in Eastern Europe

John S. Garland

Financing Foreign Trade in Eastern Europe

Problems of Bilateralism and Currency Inconvertibility

PRAEGER SPECIAL STUDIES IN INTERNATIONAL BUSINESS, FINANCE, AND TRADE

Praeger Publishers New York Washington London

Library of Congress Cataloging in Publication Data

Garland, John S
Financing foreign trade in Eastern Europe.

(Praeger special studies in international business, finance, and trade)
Bibliography: p. 151
Includes index.
1. Europe, Eastern—Commercial policy. 2. Finance—Europe, Eastern. 3. East-West trade (1945-) 4. Soviet ikonomicheskoĭ nzaimopomoschi. I. Title.
HF1531.G37 382.1'0947 76-24351
ISBN 0-275-23800-8

PRAEGER PUBLISHERS
111 Fourth Avenue, New York, N.Y. 10003, U.S.A.

Published in the United States of America in 1977
by Praeger Publishers, Inc.

Printed in the United States of America

To my parents

PREFACE

During the last ten years numerous, often dramatic changes occurred in the political climate of East-West relations. The use of the word detente blossomed and as quickly fell into disfavor. News coverage granted top priority to East-West political meetings. High ranking political officials as well as reporters contributed to the creation of an atmosphere of excitement by giving the impression that such political meetings would significantly change the course of future developments. Of much greater significance, however, and of much more far-reaching consequence for future East-West relations, are certain basic economic changes in Eastern Europe that have been much less widely recognized and given scarce notice in our press. The economic structure and functioning of the Council for Mutual Economic Assistance (CMEA) have been undergoing changes which, although not as superficially dramatic as those in the primarily political realm, could eventually lead to a restructuring of international economic relations on a world-wide basis.

Nevertheless, the members of the East European council for Mutual Economic Assistance (Comecon) have as yet found no feasible solution to certain limitations inherent in the twin institutions of bilateralism and currency inconvertibility, both of which are products of the economic chaos immediately following the Second World War. This book represents an attempt to determine some of the effects of bilateralism and currency inconvertibility on the financing of foreign trade in Eastern Europe. At the same time, an attempt is made to give necessary recognition to the changing political environment in which that foreign trade occurs. Following World War II, the political environment determined to a large extent the patterns of foreign trade; we are now entering an era in which the reverse is becoming more and more the case. It is for this reason that the primary emphasis in this book is economic rather than political, but the interdependence of the two remains indisputable.

My interest in this subject is the result of a graduate class in International Finance held at Wichita State University in the Fall of 1975. I wish to acknowledge my indebtedness to the inspiring teaching of Lee C. Nehrt, Professor of International Management. He not only provided the stimulus and encouragement for this work, but also assisted in preparing the manuscript form.

CONTENTS

LIST OF TABLES

LIST OF ABBREVIATIONS

CCC	Commodity Credit Corporation
CMEA	Council for Mutual Economic Assistance
Comecon	East European Council for Mutual Economic Assistance
EEC	European Economic Community
FRG	Federal Republic of Germany (West Germany)
GATT	General Agreement on Tariffs and Trade
GDR	German Democratic Republic (East Germany)
IBEC	International Bank for Economic Cooperation
IBRD	International Bank for Reconstruction and Development
IIB	International Investment Bank
IMF	International Monetary Fund
MFN	most favored nation
MNCs	multinational corporations
OECD	Organization for Economic Cooperation and Development
OPIC	Overseas Private Investment Corporation

INTRODUCTION

According to C. Fred Bergsten,[1] research on East-West trade has suffered from neglect in four major aspects. First, in relation to its being the most highly politicized area of international economic relations, we see two extreme approaches: the political aspects are either overemphasized at the expense of economic considerations; or economists fail to factor critical political considerations into their analyses. Second, a new environment for East-West economic relations seems to be rapidly developing. Third, there has been an overemphasis in the research on trade itself, which limits the scope of research and neglects the further consideration of the evolution of financial institutions, types of agreements, and so on. Fourth, generalizations about "East" and "West" continue to dominate much of the work in the area and hinder the recognition of distinct economic and political differences among countries.

The purpose of this work is to explore certain aspects of Eastern European bilateralism, inconvertibility, and financing of foreign trade. Thus, our attention is not directly focused on East-West trade as such. To the contrary, it is felt that an evaluation of the structure and functioning of the Eastern European foreign trade apparatus itself might overcome some of the weaknesses indicated above, while still being of value to those students of East-West trade per se.

Originally, the focus of this work was to be on problems stemming from the inconvertibility of Eastern bloc currencies. The research has made obvious, however, that the problems cannot be easily isolated, and not at all properly evaluated unless due weight in the investigation is given to the related policies, institutions, and trade patterns of Comecon (the East European Council for Mutual Economic Assistance). Accordingly, the scope of the work has grown. The report begins with a brief economic analysis of Comecon to provide a background for the main investigation; thus the first section will be concerned with the role and patterns of foreign trade in the Council for Mutual Economic Assistance (CMEA), intrabloc integration and interdependence, and economic reform. It is the second section which attempts to give a general assessment of bilateralism and currency inconvertibility. Finally, attention is directed to the financing of foreign trade, with emphasis placed on credit policies and the types of financing arrangements which are necessitated under present conditions. In this final section, emphasis is placed on East-West trade arrangements.

It should be immediately pointed out that by "Eastern Europe" is meant Bulgaria, Czechoslovakia, East Germany (the GDR), Hungary, Poland, and Romania. Yugoslavia is not being considered because of its special forms of government and economy. The USSR, in spite of its dominant role in Comecon, is not being considered because its problems are quite different than those of the smaller countries; some of the effects of Russian policy on the smaller countries, however, will be referred to. Three other Comecon nations are given no consideration. Outer Mongolia need not concern us because of its being in essence, at least economically, part of the Soviet Union; Albania, although technically a Comecon member, has been virtually independent of the organization since the early 1960s, and no longer participates in the deliberations of that body.[2] Finally, although Cuba has been a member of Comecon since 1972, it is neither East European nor actually integrated within the organization to any great extent.

NOTES

1. C. Fred Bergsten, The Future of the International Economic Order: An Agenda for Research (Lexington: Heath, 1973), pp. 39-40.

2. James A. Ramsey, "The 'Euroruble' -- Competition or Convertibility?," Columbia Journal of World Business 3 (November-December 1968): 65.

Financing Foreign Trade in Eastern Europe

PART

I

BACKGROUND NOTES ON COMECON

INTRODUCTION

Since its creation in 1949, the Council for Mutual Economic Assistance (CMEA) has undergone four phases: a dormant phase until 1955; an activation phase from then until 1962; a consolidation phase between 1963 and 1968; and a reactivation phase after 1968.[1] It is this fourth phase, which is intended to focus on a 15 to 20 year period of economic integration, in which we are primarily interested. According to the Comecon Charter,

> "The purpose of the Council for Mutual Economic Assistance is to promote, by uniting and coordination the efforts of the member countries of the Council, the planned development of the national economy, the acceleration of economic and technical progress in these countries, the raising of the level of industrialization in the industrially less-developed countries, a steady increase in the productivity of labour and a constant improvement in the welfare of the peoples of the member countries of the Council."[2]

The charter, signed in 1960, was extended by the "Basic Principles of Socialist Cooperation" of 1962, a policy statement which somewhat changed the original purpose, at least in depth: the 1962 statement calls for specialization according to comparative advantages, and for joint planning for the CMEA area as a whole, thus calling for a supranational planning authority.[3]

Sandor Ausch, a Hungarian socialist, has claimed that the CMEA has proved vastly superior in several significant aspects to its capitalist counterparts:

> "Perhaps the most important of all changes was that, in the framework of the new system, long-term agreements have opened up, and guaranteed, markets to the mutual commodity exports of all these countries, among them some rather underdeveloped ones, which just started industrialization and were endowed with relatively small areas and domestic markets. It is a

> statistical fact that these latter countries have been transacting ever since much larger net exports of finished goods than any capitalist country at a comparable level of economic development. At the same time, most of the raw materials needed for their rapidly growing industries could be purchased in the framework of guaranteed supplies. All this contributed to reducing the deficit in the balance of international payments, most characteristically associated with economic growth in this stage of development, thus enabling these countries to avoid many of the well-known economic and political consequences of such deficit."[4]

In view of this contention, it must be pointed out that CMEA policies have in many ways been detrimental to the expansion of export markets and that they in fact have contributed to severe balance-of-payments problems, as we shall later discover. Be that as it may, it would be advantageous at this point to determine the role and patterns of Comecon foreign trade before we look more closely at CMEA integration.

NOTES

1. Henry Wilcox Schaefer, Comecon and the Politics of Integration (New York: Praeger, 1972), p. vii.
2. "The Comecon Charter," in Comecon: Integration Problems of the Planned Economies, ed. Michael Kaser (New York: Oxford University, 1967), p. 236.
3. Jozef M. P. van Brabant, Bilateralism and Structural Bilateralism in Intra-CMEA Trade (Rotterdam: Rotterdam University Press, 1973), pp. 9-10.
4. Sandor Ausch, Theory and Practice of CMEA Cooperation (Budapest: Akademiai Kiado, 1972), p. 11.

CHAPTER 1
THE ROLE AND PATTERNS OF CMEA FOREIGN TRADE

THE ROLE OF FOREIGN TRADE

Alan A. Brown sees an inherent contradiction between the socialist policy of autarky and the dynamic trade pattern that can be expected to emerge in a centrally planned economy.[1] Basically, he sees two sets of factors, one tending to lower, the other to raise the equilibrium level of trade in a centrally planned economy relative to a similar type market economy. The effects of the first set, the thesis, are termed trade aversion; those of the second, or antithesis, are termed trade proclivity. The synthesis emerges through the interaction of the two, and is termed trade ambivalence, alluding to the difficulty of attaining a stable equilibrium in the level, composition, and direction of trade.

Trade aversion results from those variables which tend to increase the implicit costs of trade (cost sensitivity), and/or those which tend to reduce the explicit benefits from trade (benefit denial). The noneconomic factors of cost sensitivity include the danger of foreign trade to national independence or security, and the conflict with Marxian ideology. The economic factors of cost sensitivity are connected with the problems of planning and control, arising principally from the transmission of external fluctuations and the increased complexity of planning and control, the first of which is due primarily to the influence of the world market mechanism. There are basically two causes of trade proclivity: the emphasis on rapid industrial growth, and the use of foreign trade as an external safety valve.

Trade ambivalence, or the difficulty of maintaining equilibrium, arises through the interaction of exports and imports, as well as from the conflicts already mentioned. When the need arises to mobilize more exports, the planners are apt to turn to domestic low-priority goods which are thought to be least difficult to withdraw from domestic markets. This, however, causes a change in priorities as such, and weakens the priority system on which it is based. Additionally, quality suffers due to the unaccustomed demand placed on low-priority goods, whose quality control is already and understandably rather lax. This in turn leads to a decline of export prices and a deterioration of the terms of trade. All this is complicated by the fact that the traditional neglect of low-priority industries, the lack of investment, obsolete equipment and technical skills, retards their technical progress and reduces their rate of productivity improvement, if not absolutely, at least relative to other sectors.

As we shall see, foreign trade is of vital importance to the countries under consideration. Both the goals and limits of foreign trade are determined by the directing bodies of the state economy. The main objective of foreign trade is to procure goods and services which are both indispensable and unavailable from domestic sources. Of only secondary consideration are those goods and services which can be produced at home, but can be obtained by international exchange more advantageously; in this case, other than economic concerns enter the picture, and home production might be demanded, even under unfavorable conditions, in order to develop productive forces internally. At any rate, in the centrally planned economies it is imports which are the goal, with exports being only the means to pay for them.[2]

The role of foreign trade has thus been viewed not as an opportunity to benefit the CMEA countries through specialization, but rather to assure the inputs when economic requirements exceed domestic supply. In such a case, which is nearly a chronic condition due to the socialist policy of overemployment, the needed imports are often gained through the bartering of whatever domestic supplies are in short-run excess supply. Since autarky has been a policy of some significance to these countries, foreign trade has been viewed as a source of potential disruption to planning. Although such a view is not totally unrealistic for the Soviet Union, which is vast and diversified, it is completely unrealistic for the smaller countries of East Europe, which copied the USSR's planning practices.[3] In short, this places exports in a completely subordinate position to that of imports, with the two being highly interdependent.

Actually, Soviet influence on Comecon policy has in this sense been extremely detrimental to the smaller members. Not only is the USSR much larger and diversified enough not to be dependent on foreign trade, but it has long been relatively isolated from the capitalist world, of which the other Eastern European members of Comecon were historically a part. Part of the conflict stems from the assumptions which underlie the deterministic and voluntaristic theories of modernization and development. Whereas the Western world has based its assumptions on deterministic theory, which stresses the impersonal forces of market mechanisms, socialist theory stresses voluntaristic action, which places much more emphasis on the decisive role of human consciousness. In other words, whereas capitalist economies develop and evolve, the socialist economies are built.[4]

The relative difference in the importance of trade to the USSR and the smaller Comecon members is clearly indicated by noting the ratio of exports to national income: 35 percent for Hungary, 30 percent for Czechoslovakia, 28 percent for Bulgaria, 25 percent for East Germany, but only 4 percent for the Soviet Union. Such high dependence on foreign trade puts extreme pressure on the economy's planners, is very costly in view of balance-of-payments deficits, and places the country in direct and serious competition with countries of the industrialized West.[5]

Another indication of the dependence on foreign trade by East Europe is given by considering the 1971 import levels as a percentage of GNP. For Bulgaria it was 16.2 percent, for Czechoslovakia 11.7 percent, for East Germany 12.1 percent, for Hungary 17.6 percent, for Poland 8.2 percent, for Romania 7.8 percent, and for the USSR only 2.2 percent.[6] When one considers Comecon foreign trade as a whole, the figures are thus extremely misleading, due to the Soviet Union's influence on the total figures. Comecon as a whole, for instance, is responsible for 30 percent of the world's total industrial output, although it participates in only 10 percent of world trade.[7] Nevertheless, as we have noted, foreign trade is in fact a crucial part of national economic planning for the smaller members of Comecon because of the need to acquire exchange earnings to pay for essential imports.

Still, the ratio of foreign trade to national income is generally lower in the CMEA countries than in the capitalist countries of comparable size and level of economic development. Part of the reason for this lies in the fact that market mechanisms are eliminated to a large extent in the CMEA planning considerations, which leads to protectionism and autarkic economic policy. In addition, there are structural factors, which are related to the members' having surpluses or deficits in the same kind of commodities, and to bilateralism, which also limits the expansion of CMEA's foreign trade.[8]

The autarkic tendencies of the CMEA countries were particularly strong during the first years of the organization, and due largely to the influence of Stalin's policies, which were shaped by, among other things, historic experience with wide fluctuations in capitalist markets, hostility with the Western countries, and the desire for industrialization to achieve a balanced economic structure in traditionally agricultural countries. When the smaller countries adopted the Soviet model of self-sufficiency, foreign trade became a necessary evil to facilitate industrialization. Since the mid-1950s, however, the autarkic ideals have been giving way more and more to the economic needs of the member states, which have in general a narrow raw material base and small domestic markets. Indeed, since the Korean War the value of CMEA foreign trade has been rising faster than that of the capitalist world.[9]

Nevertheless, foreign trade is definitely stifled in the centrally planned economies, for, according to Sandor Ausch,

> ". . . in the individual national economies the very existence of an economic system based on direct plan instructions necessarily involves such international economic relations, such a type of world market and world economy as will either totally and absolutely hinder the functioning of the categories of commodity, value and money, or else, force them to assume forms which, instead of ensuring a gradual unfolding of the advantages stemming from the international division of labour, act exactly against the utilization of these advantages to an extent that will even grow parallel with the process of development."[10]

In our consideration of the patterns of foreign trade of the CMEA countries, it is advisable to distinguish between intra-CMEA trade, trade with the West, and trade with the less-developed countries. Such distinction is far from arbitrary, for the institutions and accounting practices differ accordingly. Intrabloc trade is mostly conducted through arbitrary and conventional accounting units in the hope of achieving better coordination of total industrialization efforts; trade with the West is generally based on prices established by competitive market mechanisms; and trade with the underdeveloped countries is usually financed on the basis of bilateral clearing arrangements.[11]

THE PATTERNS OF FOREIGN TRADE

Intrabloc Trade

The economic integration of Comecon has undergone three stages as far as trade patterns are concerned. During the first stage, which lasted until 1955, the individual economies were all tied to that of the Soviet Union through a series of bilateral agreements and actions, reflecting V. M. Molotov's answer to the Marshall Plan. The second stage, with some overlapping, and lasting until 1959, emphasized the development of intrabloc trade in which a network of bilateral agreements was established among all CMEA members. The third stage was prompted by the Sino-Soviet split in 1959, and is generally characterized by intensified efforts of the Soviets aimed at achieving rapid and total integration of the economies of the Comecon nations.[12] Such efforts will be considered in a later section of this work, when we investigate the aspects of Comecon integration. We are primarily interested in determining the foreign trade patterns of the Comecon nations to provide a background for the later, more thorough consideration.

The data in Appendix Tables A-1 through A-8 indicate quite convincingly, in terms of trade as a percentage of total trade and as a percentage of net material product, how heavily dependent the Eastern European countries are on their economic ties with the USSR and with other bloc countries. As we shall discover later, the causal relationship between CMEA institutions and intrabloc trade works in both directions. That is, although increased intrabloc trade is a result of the changes within the CMEA institutions, those organizational changes were themselves to a large extent fostered by the increased trade itself. Since the bilateral agreements became more and more obvious in their limitations, the growth in trade demanded new relationships among the individual members, and a greater role for money not only as a means of payment, but as a measure of value and a means of accumulating currency reserves.[13]

There has been a change also in the concept of socialist autarky. It appears as if the Eastern policy of autarky no longer means self-sufficiency for the individual bloc member, but rather for Comecon collectively. Whatever the case, two-thirds of the present volume of foreign trade by the members as a whole is kept within the bloc. Without doubt, the member countries have diverted trade toward each other and away from the outside world, since the level of such trade in 1948 was no more than 30 percent. The set of restrictive forces which has hampered East-West trade is centered, at least financially, around the inconvertibility of CMEA currencies.[14] In fact, it has been postulated by Western sources that the Comecon group intends to establish a long-term ratio of 80 percent to 20 percent between intra-Comecon trade and trade with outside countries.[15] Statistics as well as political-economic events since 1970, however, seem to clearly indicate that this will not be the case. Instead of reducing the relative percentage of East-West trade, it appears as if such trade will gradually, although certainly not drastically, reduce the overall relative importance of intrabloc trade. For one thing, CMEA is not as yet a common market with common external tariffs; in addition, internal problems, which shall be discussed later, weaken any attempts to further consolidate the organization.

Actually, Comecon intrabloc trade grew more slowly in 1966-70 than in 1961-65 (by 8.2 percent compared with 8.5 percent), and also more slowly than world trade as a whole. In respect to the latter, the volume difference is not as great as figures indicate, however, for Comecon prices were more stable than world market prices, which rose considerably. In addition, the percentage of Soviet trade with the Comecon area has gradually been falling in recent years, as indicated in Table 1.1. Earlier, common ideology, geographical proximity and the difficulty of earning foreign exchange in capitalist countries had favored intrabloc trade, which had been strengthened anyway by the Western strategic embargo (after 1947) and the Korean War (1950-53). Since then, however, the solidarity of CMEA has been weakening due to increasing political-national differences among members, relaxation of Soviet control of the smaller countries, and by the increasing attractiveness of trade with the West.[16]

Eastern European sources contend that such relative lessening of intrabloc ties does not imply any sign of disintegration of the Soviet bloc. To the contrary, it is considered to have strengthening effects through the increased sophistication of bloc industry by increased technological development and capacity. The strategy is that, instead of having its raw materials processed separately in the smaller

TABLE 1.1

Percentage Comecon Share of Soviet Foreign Trade

1965	1966	1967	1968	1969	1970
58.0	56.0	57.1	57.5	56.7	55.6

Source: "Current Developments: Comecon Trade Plans," East Europe 21 (April 1972):30.

Comecon countries, the Soviet Union should integrate their economies with its own, import advanced technology from the West and export greater numbers of simple machines and plants to the developing countries.[17]

The central position of the USSR has dominated intrabloc trade. By far the most important Soviet trading partner in Eastern Europe is East Germany, followed by Poland, Czechoslovakia, Bulgaria, Hungary and Romania. Together, Eastern Europe accounts for more than 65 percent of Soviet foreign trade.[18] Because of the bilateral nature of foreign trade within Comecon, the USSR trade puts heavy pressure on the smaller countries, as is seen from the following:[19]

	Trade within Comecon	Soviet Union's share
Bulgaria	72	two-thirds
Czechoslovakia	65	one-half
East Germany	69	two-thirds
Hungary	65	one-half
Poland	58	three-fifths
Romania	56	one-half

It can be seen that each member country transacts only a small fraction of its trade with other small members which might, theoretically, arrange production programs to serve their economic interests. Yet flexibility is not easily gained, since the system of planning used leads to inelasticities of partners' supply and demand. This, in addition to bilateralism and inconvertibility, leaves virtually no mechanisms for short-term adjustments to changing requirements, either in terms of internal plans or of balance-of-payments balances.[20] Nevertheless, indications are that the significance of USSR-bloc trade shall decrease in favor of expanded trade among the other members.

East-West Trade

The present developed capitalist countries claimed three-quarters of Eastern Europe's trade before World War II, a share which dropped to 15 percent during the Korean War. Now, with increasing interest in the mutual benefits of East-West trade, the share has risen to 25 percent. The Eastern bloc countries have found that as they reach higher levels of economic development, their need of trade with the West increases instead of diminishes.[21]

For decades, discussions of East-West trade were highly emotion-laden. Recently, more objective analyses seem to be forthcoming.

For instance, the reduction of economic barriers is no longer accepted as automatically fostering harmonious intercountry relations, since it has been recognized that liberalization along those lines could in fact lead to new political frictions, especially between countries which have had very little economic interchange: economically integrated blocs are no longer considered inherently bad.[22]

When at first the reduction of political tensions inspired an increase in the volume of East-West trade, most observers felt that trade was increasingly being dictated by economics rather than by politics. Current thinking is probably more accurate: that what has occurred seems to be "less a depoliticization of the issue-area than a change in the political orientations of the major actors and therefore in the types of linkages that they are willing to insist on and the agreements that can be reached."[23] That is, trade is not equally valued by both sides; regardless of detente, trade decisions remain highly politicized by the very nature of central planning; and residual ideological and security differences remain significant.[24]

Table 1.2 shows the rapid increase of trade between Eastern Europe and the European Economic Community (EEC), its largest customer in the West. In spite of such favorable developments, political considerations still hinder the expansion of such trade. In September 1975, China became the only communist nation besides Yugoslavia to establish diplomatic relations with the Common Market, with which the Eastern European nations have no direct dealings.[25] On its part, the EEC does not consider Comecon as a supranational organization, a result of an EEC legal study of Comecon's jurisdiction vis-a-vis third countries,[26] and a fact which handicaps

TABLE 1.2

Soviet Bloc Trade With Common Market, 1958 and 1968
(millions of dollars)

	Exports to Common Market		Imports from Common Market		Turnover	
	1958	1968	1958	1968	1958	1968
Eastern Europe	430	1,300	415	1,580	845	2,880
USSR	270	760	205	800	475	1,560
Total bloc	700	2,060	620	2,380	1,320	4,440

Source: Reprinted from The Communist Regimes in Eastern Europe by Richard F. Staar with the permission of the publishers, Hoover Institution Press. Copyright © 1971 by the Board of Trustees of the Leland Stanford Junior University.

TABLE 1.3

Share of East European Countries' Exports and Imports To and From the West in 1970 (percent of total)

	Exports to			Imports from		
	Developed Countries (1)	Less Developed Countries (2)	1 & 2	Developed Countries (4)	Less Developed Countries (5)	4 & 5
Bulgaria	16.0	7.7	23.7	20.1	6.7	26.8
Czechoslovakia	24.4	9.8	34.2	27.4	7.7	35.1
East Germany	23.8	5.6	29.4	27.8	5.0	32.8
Hungary	31.0	6.0	37.0	31.6	6.3	37.9
Poland	30.3	7.8	38.1	27.5	5.7	33.2
Romania	34.5	10.5	45.0	40.9	7.4	48.3

Source: E. Amid-hozour and J. Somogyi, "East-West Trade," Finance and Development 10 (June 1973): 35.

those trying to establish closer economic relations between the two blocs. The EEC plan calls for the EEC Commission, as sole negotiator for the EEC, to hammer out trade agreements with individual Comecon countries; the Comecon proposal of February 1976 calls for bloc-to-bloc agreements delineating the scope of economic and trade cooperation, including such specifics as standardization, environment, economic forecasts and statistics. The basic conflict is that Comecon wants bilateral trade conventions between individual Comecon countries and each EEC member state to implement a general agreement, whereas the EEC seeks agreements between each individual Comecon country and the EEC as an entity.[27] It is felt in Western European circles that the pressure applied by the Comecon proposal is a Soviet tactic to politically embarrass the EEC in front of the Comecon member states, several of which have been flirting recently with the idea of acting individually vis-a-vis the Common Market.[28]

The fact is, East-West trade is much more vital to the Eastern European countries than to the West, for such trade represents 30 percent of their total trade, although only about 3.5 percent of the West's total trade. Naturally, its significance varies markedly among individual countries, as is indicated in Table 1.3. In 1970 the East

European countries' share of exports with the West ranged from 23 percent to 45 percent, the highest for Romania and Poland, and the lowest for the Soviet Union and Bulgaria. Imports follow a similar pattern, as indicated. In 1970-71, practically all developed countries increased their imports from Eastern Europe in about the same proportion as their total import growth. One feature of such recent trade, however, has been an increase in the import surplus of East European countries coupled with a corresponding increase in trade credit to these countries,[29] a development to which we shall refer later.

Bloc Trade with the Developing Countries

The Eastern bloc's share of the total trade of the developing countries amounted to little over 5 percent in 1964, and has been gaining substantially. However, since the bloc's trade with the developing countries is concentrated on a relatively few countries, the effect is much stronger in certain areas. Comecon as a group has a higher level of trade with the developing countries than does the USSR. Czechoslovakia, having trade agreements with over 30 developing countries, ranks first among the countries of Eastern Europe in such trade, and accounts for roughly one-third of their trade with the developing countries. Poland and East Germany are in second place, each accounting for roughly one-fifth of this trade.[30]

Actually, in spite of the small relative amount of trade with the developing countries, such trade is much more significant to the Eastern European countries than might be assumed, since its nature is quite different from the trade with the industrialized West. For one thing, the Comecon countries usually have a surplus in their balance of trade with these countries. Even more important, however, is the advantageous structure of the trade. Bulgaria offers a good example of this. Bulgaria's exports to the developing countries consist of comparatively large shares of machinery and equipment. These are not only the most profitable of Bulgaria's exports, but the market is of vital interest to the Bulgarian machinery industry while it is still in its infant stage. This allows time to develop, mature, and reach international standards, all of which must be done before penetration of those markets requiring higher quality.[31]

Statistics of East European exports and imports to the less-developed countries are found in Tables 1.4 and 1.5. The USSR is in a unique position among Comecon nations in regard to trade with the developing countries, as shown by Table 1.6; it is the only member of the bloc to carry deficits, whereas the other Comecon nations were carrying surpluses (between 1955 and 1964).

TABLE 1.4

Estimated Exports from Communist Countries to Developing Countries, 1955-64
(millions of U.S. dollars)

Country	1955	1956	1957	1958	1959	1960	1961	1962	1963	1964
Bulgaria	5.2	11.3	17.7	13.0	14.4	23.7	25.6	39.7	50.4	64.4
Czechoslovakia	177.4	245.9	213.9	208.2	201.1	226.2	283.8	249.9	240.6	269.8
East Germany	62.1	65.5	101.8	98.6	98.8	121.9	137.6	128.3	144.1	173.2
Hungary	57.7	40.8	41.9	51.3	57.5	65.9	76.0	78.5	92.0	97.2
Poland	74.7	78.1	78.6	126.2	114.3	123.8	148.3	148.7	162.2	194.0
Romania	37.8	34.7	25.0	32.1	32.7	48.4	51.2	75.0	67.1	82.0

Source: Carole A. Sawyer, Communist Trade With Developing Countries: 1955-65 (New York: Praeger, 1966), p. 19.

TABLE 1.5

Estimated Imports by Communist Countries From Developing Countries, 1955-64
(millions of U.S. dollars)

Country	1955	1956	1957	1958	1959	1960	1961	1962	1963	1964
Bulgaria	3.2	9.0	12.9	11.7	11.1	15.1	19.2	34.5	35.6	58.8
Czechoslovakia	133.0	139.9	145.1	152.6	178.8	198.4	235.3	195.0	218.6	214.9
East Germany	51.8	66.7	112.4	120.4	106.7	134.2	105.7	115.4	121.3	166.6
Hungary	53.5	36.0	28.2	41.1	46.6	54.0	58.0	75.0	91.4	120.2
Poland	84.5	50.3	70.9	80.7	97.4	112.8	104.4	127.2	149.7	178.2
Romania	22.3	19.6	21.7	25.8	23.6	26.6	44.3	51.6	62.9	58.9

Source: Carole A. Sawyer, Communist Trade With Developing Countries: 1955-65 (New York: Praeger, 1966), p. 20.

TABLE 1.6

Estimated Trade Balances of the USSR and Eastern Europe with Developing Countries, 1955-64
(millions of U.S. dollars)

Year	USSR	Eastern Europe
1955	-98.1	66.8
1956	-117.0	154.9
1957	-152.5	87.8
1958	-92.3	97.1
1959	-178.7	54.5
1960	-229.1	68.7
1961	-76.9	155.2
1962	-46.7	121.4
1963	86.0	77.1
1964	114.8	83.0

Source: Carole A. Sawyer, Communist Trade With Developing Countries, 1955-65 (New York: Praeger, 1966), p. 21.

THE BALANCE OF PAYMENTS

In centrally planned economies, the central plan most generally equalizes imports and exports. In fact, the very need for imports creates the need for exports. In any case, if the central planning functions as intended, there is no need for a special mechanism equilibrating the balance of payments, such as exchange rate changes of the public sector's international reserves. That is, as long as the central plan operates smoothly and governs tightly, the level of foreign reserves in a centrally planned economy is irrelevant to its ability to pay for a given level of imports.[32] On the other hand, no theory is better than the practice which it implies. As we shall discover, every single country under consideration has found it necessary to implement changes in the form of economic reforms. To the extent that the economic planning is becoming liberalized, balance-of-payments problems can, and in fact do, arise, but are no longer considered inherently damaging.

In general, the circulation of money in the East European states has three characteristic features: a strict separation of foreign payments from the domestic money circulation, the carrying out of intrabloc trade on the basis of strict bilateral clearing, and a sharp distinction between cash (for payments between individuals) and money on account (for payments between public authorities and enterprises). Thus changes in the balance of payments cannot influence the domestic monetary situation directly through monetary operations. That is, foreign payments problems cannot directly affect either the rate of exchange or the relations and the level of domestic prices.[33]

The concept of the market balance of payments thus loses its relevance in a socialist economy. Instead, there is a programmed balance of payments, represented by the list of requirements (imports) which must be satisfied according to the priority established, and the satisfaction of which must be dependent on the level of exports. If there is a surplus, imports or reserves of foreign exchange may be increased. In the case of a deficit, if credits cannot be obtained and gold is not available for export, either imports must be reduced or goods and services withdrawn from the domestic supply and sold abroad. Such a method of balancing payments is swift and effective, but inefficient if the country must call upon other members of Comecon to accept the additional exports needed. In such a case, the trading partner realizes his strategic advantage over the exporting country, in addition to being asked to accept goods not already provided for in the national plan. Because the partner is in such a good position to improve his terms of trade, the existence of a free world market continues to play an important role for the centrally planned economies.[34]

One balance-of-payments problem seems to be unique to centrally planned economies, and that is their chronic practice of "taut" or overfull employment planning, which means that planned demand exceeds available supply. Accordingly, domestic producers and consumers fight for exportables and more imports, thereby creating pressures in the direction of balance-of-payments deterioration.[35]

Although CMEA countries have not generally revealed their balance-of-payments positions, data have been pieced together from various sources which allow us to estimate the hard-currency position of CMEA countries. Still, the question remains concerning the ability of the Comecon nations to service their debts. Whatever the case, while invisible earnings and credits offer scope for increasing the import capacity of East European countries, export performance will be the major factor.[36] At the beginning of 1974, the total gross indebtedness to the West of the USSR and the six European CMEA countries was estimated at between $14 and $16 billion, of which the USSR accounted for between $5.1 and $6.6 billion, and the countries under consideration for from $9 to $10 billion. Since their volume of exports to the West in 1973 was about $8.5 billion ($3 billion by the

USSR, $5.5 billion by the others), the gross indebtedness to the industrial West for CMEA as a whole was close to twice the size of its exports to the same area. This of course varies from country to country, with the ratio of indebtedness to exports higher than the average for Bulgaria and Romania. Complicating the analysis by Western sources is the fact that they do not know the extent of hard-currency assets among these countries, which is estimated to be several million dollars excluding the USSR, which has considerable gold holdings.[37]

It should be pointed out, however, that, although the burden of indebtedness of two given countries might appear similar relative to the volume of exports of those countries, the impact of indebtedness on the domestic economy may be quite dissimilar. The reliance on exports is quite heavy for the smaller countries, as we have repeatedly pointed out, while for the USSR the foreign sector is relatively quite small. Thus the availability and servicing of credits have a much greater impact on the countries under consideration than they do for the Soviet Union. The significance of indebtedness also depends upon the growth rate of debts relative to exports (during the last decade, each CMEA country's debts have grown much faster than exports); reserve position; composition of the debt (short-, medium-, and long-term; prospects for increasing the debtor's hard-currency earnings through commodity and invisibles exports); and continued availability of new financing. In all these respects, there are significant differences among the individual Comecon nations. The countries under consideration have in general only modest to insignificant hard currency and gold reserves, and, except for Romania, do not produce gold or knowingly possess significant gold deposits. Eastern European countries, in general, earn hard currency by exporting primary products, semimanufactures, and foodstuffs to the industrial West, although East Germany and Czechoslovakia are in a relatively much better position as far as the composition of exports is concerned. Another weakness is found in the fact that, with the exception of Poland, these countries are generally poorly endowed with fuels and other raw materials which are rapidly increasing in world-wide demand.[38]

Table 1.7 provides a breakdown of the composition of the estimated indebtedness of the six countries under consideration, an indebtedness which reached $7 billion by the end of 1971. At that time, about one-fourth of the total debt was comprised of medium- and long-term suppliers' credits, most of which were backed by government guarantees. Since the mid-1950s, however, commercial bank credits have grown in importance, and now account for over one-half of the total indebtedness. The remaining one-fourth is composed of short-

TABLE 1.7

Estimated Composition of the Total Indebtedness of the Six Eastern European Countries, December 31, 1971

Type of Indebtedness	Amount ($ billion)	Percent of Total
Initial Indebtedness		
(January 1, 1959)	0.4	6
Supplier Credits:		
medium- and long-term(government guaranteed and other)	1.8	26
short-term	0.4	6
Agricultural Credits:		
PL 480 (Poland)	0.4	6
Commodity Credit Corporation	0.1	1
Commercial Bank Credits (including some nonguaranteed supplier credits)	3.6	51
Swing Credits (intra-German trade)	0.1	1
Total Indebtedness	7.0	100

Source: Reprinted by permission of the publisher, from Changing Perspectives In East-West Commerce, edited by Carl H. McMillan (Lexington, Mass.: Lexington Books, D.C. Heath and Company, 1974), p. 130.

term supplier credits and special sources. Since 1971, other sources of credit are gaining in significance, a development which we shall discuss later. It has been approximated that the debt of the countries under consideration has increased from $7 to $9.4 billion during 1972 and 1973.[39]

The CMEA countries have chronically suffered from shortages of foreign exchange. This stems from both supply and demand conditions. On the demand side, there is a growing need for imports of industrial equipment due to the planned rapid industrialization, nonfulfillment of targets (which then must be made good by imports), low quality of domestic production and unsatisfied consumer demand. On the supply side, the development is not usually geared to build up export capacity due to the emphasis on autarky, the prevailing seller's market at home (which reduces the inclination to export), discrimination of all sorts in capitalist markets, and general deterioration of quality because of the "softness" of East European markets (referred to by Ljubo Sirc as "the Comecon effect").[40] This being the case, CMEA imports, especially from the industrialized West, are conditioned not so much by demand, but by the fluctuating export earnings and low reserves held.[41]

Accordingly, balance-of-payments considerations on the part of the Eastern bloc nations tend to inhibit imports, particularly since these countries are either unwilling or unable to divert significant quantities of gold, to take advantage of the International Monetary Fund's (IMF) special drawing rights, to employ hard currencies earned elsewhere, or to sustain persistent bilateral trade deficits.[42] On the other hand, the chronic shortage of foreign exchange reserves has not prevented early repayment of foreign debt obligations, nor has it interrupted the Eastern bloc's substantial economic aid programs to lesser developed nations. Even though such aid is generally in the form of goods and credit instead of convertible currencies, it indirectly reduces export earnings from elsewhere.[43]

COMMODITY STRUCTURE OF EXPORTS AND IMPORTS

In addition to the nature of bilateralism, which we shall discuss in detail in a later chapter, there are other impediments to the export capacity of the East European countries. Quite simply, their production is not well adjusted to the production of goods suitable to meet the demand in external markets, especially in the developed countries. The range of products is limited, quality often fails to meet foreign requirements, marketing and servicing facilities are not fully developed, and the limited availability of export credit further hinders the abilities of the Eastern countries to compete on the world market. Moreover, the Western countries are sophisticated in their shopping. Because their import demands are rapidly changing, the East European countries, with centralized longer-range planning, are not well adapted to producing for such markets. Both managerial skill and experience in foreign marketing, as well as the necessary flexibility, are also lacking.[44]

Industrial goods of the CMEA countries have also encountered marketing difficulties within their own bloc. Even when they are up to bloc standards, there is a lack of demand, particularly for conventional industrial machinery. This is due in large part to the overcapacity to manufacture similar products, a condition which has grown directly from earlier Comecon expansion policies.[45]

Eighty percent of East European imports from the developed countries in 1970 were manufactured goods, mainly machinery and equipment; 56 percent of East European exports to the developed countries were raw materials. Not surprisingly, the commodity structure of trade with the developing countries was just the reverse. Seventy-seven percent of East European exports to these countries consisted of manufactures, whereas 85 percent of the imports were raw materials.[46]

It is basically the stress on rapid industrialization at the expense of consumer goods that has caused the imports from the West to consist primarily of capital equipment, technology, and industrial raw materials. Still, periodic agricultural shortages due to poor crop years have led the CMEA to import considerable amounts of grain and wheat from the West in recent years. Gradually, per capita consumption in the East is increasing, as evidenced by the 33 percent increase which had been forecasted for Poland from 1971-75.[47] With rising real income in the Comecon nations, in addition to the gradual shift in emphasis from investment to consumption, the demand for imports, and therefore the necessity of exports, is surely bound to increase.

There has been a noticeable technological lag in the industrialization of the countries under consideration. In the early stages of industrialization, planners had failed to take advantage of their investments by insisting upon the latest technological developments. Such failure was a result of the availability of cheap labor as well as of the lack of competition and availability of products from the West, created by Western discrimination. Under these circumstances, it was much more feasible to use older models and techniques. Furthermore, output maximization stressed quantitative rather than qualitative measurements, and cost efficiency became only a secondary consideration.[48]

The whole decade of the 1960s differed considerably from that of the 1950s as far as external economic relations of the Comecon nations were concerned. One significant indication of that is to be found in the export and import elasticities, that is, the comparison of export and import growth with the increase in national income. Only in the case of Romania was the importance of export demand smaller in the 1960s than in the previous decade. On the other hand, the import intensity of economic development had increased in four countries, especially in Czechoslovakia and Hungary. In Bulgaria and East Germany the import requirements of economic growth were somewhat smaller than before. The import and export elasticities are noted in Table 1.8. What the figures do not reveal, however, is

TABLE 1.8

Changes in Export and Import Elasticities

	Import Elasticities			Export Elasticities		
	1951-55	1956-60	1961-65	1951-55	1956-60	1961-65
Bulgaria	1.30	2.09	2.03	1.47	2.02	2.04
Czechoslovakia	1.28	1.66	4.20	1.05	1.49	3.57
East Germany	1.97	1.93	1.40	2.53	1.69	1.91
Hungary	1.90	1.82	2.02	2.05	1.20	2.52
Poland	1.23	1.57	1.59	0.91	1.21	1.84
Romania	0.99	1.01	1.20	1.06	1.62	1.01

Source: Reprinted from "Exports and Export Performance," by Mihaly Simai in Foreign Trade In a Planned Economy, ed. Imre Vajda and Mihaly Simai (New York: Cambridge University Press, 1971), p. 114.

that the elasticities differed not only from country to country, but from sector to sector within any given country.[49]

Because of the commodity structural imbalance of exports and imports, as already noted, a "structural stagnation" has occurred. In the long run, the ability of the Eastern bloc countries to expand trade and foreign exchange earnings is dependent upon their exporting of industrial goods. This, however, can only be accomplished if production meets Western standards. The dilemma lies in the fact that their ability to do that is itself a function of foreign trade. Such a dilemma is, of course, complicated by the present stage of industrialization, in which the USSR must serve as the primary market for their inferior goods, as well as the supplier of most of the goods necessary for industrial production.[50] Another complicating factor in the commodity structure is what we have already alluded to: whereas the industrialized West has only a limited market for the goods it imports from CMEA, Comecon demand for imports from developed countries is both high and consistent. Such imbalance of demand is definitely reaching its limits. An example is offered in the case of West Germany, one of Comecon's major Western trading partners. After West German-Comecon trade increased 22 percent during the first half of 1975, the West German Minister of Economics announced that further expansion of such trade is completely impossible unless more imports from the Eastern bloc were forthcoming, a condition which he maintains can be met only through improved quality of Eastern goods.[51]

NOTES

1. Alan A. Brown, "Towards A Theory of Centrally Planned Foreign Trade," in International Trade and Central Planning, ed. Alan A. Brown and Egon Neuberger (Los Angeles: University of California, 1968), pp. 58-103.

2. Elisabeth L. Tamedly, Socialism and International Economic Order (Caldwell: Caxton, 1969), p. 106.

3. Richard E. Caves and Ronald W. Jones, World Trade and Payments (Boston: Little, Brown, 1973), pp. 304-05.

4. Vernon V. Aspaturian, "Marxism and the Meanings of Modernization," in The Politics of Modernization in Eastern Europe, ed. Charles Gati (New York: Praeger, 1974), p. 13.

5. Gregory Grossman, "Foreign Trade, Economic Reform, and Technology," in East-West Trade and the Technology Gap: A Political and Economic Appraisal, ed. Stanislaw Wasowski (New York: Praeger, 1970), pp. 151-52.

6. James C. Baker, "United States Business Opportunities in East Europe," in China, the U.S.S.R. and Eastern Europe: A U.S. Trade Perspective, ed. John K. Ryans, Jr., Anant R. Negandhi, and James C. Baker (Kent: Kent State University, 1974), p. 104. The significant difference in percentage levels of exports and imports is due to the fact that the export figures stem from CMEA sources, whereas the import figures stem from Western sources, and are based on different accounting procedures. Here, the difference is not so important, since the stress is on the relative dependence on foreign trade of the smaller CMEA countries compared to that of the USSR.

7. Adolf Hermann, "Can Comecon Integrate?," East Europe 18 (May 1969): 15.

8. Sandor Ausch, Theory and Practice of CMEA Cooperation (Budapest: Akademiai Kiado, 1972), p. 111.

9. J. Wilczynski, The Economics of Socialism (London: Allen and Unwin, 1970), pp. 174, 177.

10. Ausch, op. cit., pp. 12-13.

11. John P. Morgan, "The Financial Aspects of East-West Trade," Columbia Journal of World Business 8 (Winter 1973): 53.

12. Glen Alden Smith, Soviet Foreign Trade: Organization, Operations, and Policy, 1918-1971 (New York: Praeger, 1973), pp. 27-28.

13. Ibid., p. 151.

14. Caves and Jones, op. cit., p. 305.
15. James R. Basche, Jr., East-West Trade: The Lessons From Experience (New York: Conference Board, 1971), p. 21.
16. Wilczynski, op. cit., p. 177.
17. Adolf Hermann, "East-West Trade: What Happens in the '70s?," East Europe 19 (November 1970): 15.
18. Douglas Evans, The Politics of Trade: The Evolution of the Superbloc (New York: Wiley and Sons, 1974), p. 39.
19. Hermann, "Can Comecon Integrate?," op. cit., p. 16.
20. Franklyn D. Holzman, Foreign Trade Under Central Planning (Cambridge: Harvard University, 1974), p. 108.
21. Wilczynski, op. cit., p. 179.
22. C. Fred Bergsten, The Future of the International Economic Order: An Agenda for Research (Lexington: Heath, 1973), pp. 14-15, 32.
23. Robert O. Keohane and Joseph S. Nye, "World Politics and the International Economic System," in The Future of the International Economic Order: An Agenda for Research, ed. C. Fred Bergsten (Lexington: Heath, 1973), p. 158.
24. Ibid., p. 160.
25. "Mainland China Begins Common Market Ties," Wall Street Journal, September 16, 1975, p. 10.
26. "Current Developments: EEC Documents on Comecon," East Europe 23 (July 1974): 28.
27. "Political Hurdles Stall Expansion of EEC-Comecon Trade," Business International 23 (February 17, 1976): 71.
28. "Test aus Moskau," Der Spiegel 10 (March 1, 1976): 105.
29. E. Amid-hozour and J. Somogyi, "East-West Trade," Finance and Development 10 (June 1973): 37.
30. Carole A. Sawyer, Communist Trade With Developing Countries, 1955-65 (New York: Praeger, 1966), p. 9.
31. Bogoslav Dobrin, Bulgarian Economic Development Since World War II (New York: Praeger, 1973), pp. 113-14.
32. Gunter Dufey, "Financing East-West Business," Columbia Journal of World Business 9 (Spring 1974): 39.
33. Wolfgang Schmitz, "Monetary Dynamic Forces in East and West: Important Developments in the Seventies," in Convertibility, Multilateralism, and Freedom, ed. Wolfgang Schmitz (New York: Springer, 1972), p. 227.
34. Tamedly, op. cit., pp. 182-83.
35. Franklyn D. Holzman, "Future East-West Economic Issues," in The Future of the International Economic Order: An Agenda for Research, ed. C. Fred Bergsten (Lexington: Heath, 1973), p. 274.

36. Geoffrey Tyler and Hubert Neiss, "Problems and Prospects in East-West Trade," Finance and Development 10 (September 1973): 24-26.

37. Carl H. McMillan, Changing Perspectives In East-West Commerce (Lexington: Heath, 1974), p. 126.

38. Ibid., pp. 126-27.

39. Ibid., p. 129.

40. Ljubo Sirc, Economic Devolution in Eastern Europe (New York: Praeger, 1969), p. 110.

41. Wilczynski, op. cit., pp. 183-84.

42. Samuel Pisar, Coexistence and Commerce (New York: McGraw-Hill, 1970), pp. 77-78.

43. Douglas R. Bohi, "An Evaluation of the Role of Eximbank and Its Promotion of East-West Trade," in U. S. Financing of East-West Trade, ed. Paul Marer (Bloomington: International Development Research Center, 1975), p. 89.

44. Tyler and Neiss, op. cit., pp. 24-26.

45. Robert W. Dean, West German Trade With the East: The Political Dimension (New York: Praeger, 1974), p. 2.

46. Amid-hozour and Somogyi, op. cit., p. 36.

47. Baker, op. cit., p. 107.

48. Dean, op. cit., p. 2.

49. Mihaly Simai, "Exports and Export Performance," in Foreign Trade In a Planned Economy, ed. Imre Vajda and Mihaly Simai (Cambridge: Cambridge University, 1971), p. 114.

50. Dean, op. cit., p. 15.

51. "Der Ost-Export steigt kraeftig," Frankfurter Allgemeine Zeitung, July 29, 1975, p. 7.

CHAPTER 2
INTRABLOC INTEGRATION AND INTERDEPENDENCE

A new phase of international cooperation of nations was introduced worldwide following the Second World War. Increasingly, the central regulating functions of autonomous national states were replaced by international organizations with varying degrees of legal sovereignty, including the field of economic and monetary affairs.[1] Now commonplace are institutions such as the International Monetary Fund (IMF), General Agreement on Tariffs and Trade (GATT), Organization for Economic Cooperation and Development (OECD), to say nothing of the European Economic Community (EEC) and other common markets and free trade areas. Each of these organizations and institutions has seen varying degrees of success. Generally speaking, in spite of many concrete achievements, the CMEA has failed to realize its goals of integration. At the heart of this failure lie the twin policies of bilateralism and inconvertibility, both of which we shall explore later. For the present, a more general picture is advisable.

At any rate, there is clearly a greater degree of economic integration in the West than among the Comecon nations. As clarified by Gottfried Haberler,

> "There is no question that bureaucratic planners and managers of public enterprises, both in the mixed economies in the West and in fully socialized, centralized or decentralized economies in the East, are much more averse to engage in international economic transactions, more conscious of national interests and constrained by national boundaries, than private,

> profit-seeking businessmen. . . . There can hardly be a doubt that despite real or alleged monopolies, oligopolies, and other deviations from perfect competition, and despite the disregard of real or imagined externalities, the 'invisible hand' of often imperfect competition, impeded though it is by tariffs and other government restrictions of trade, has managed to integrate the Western economies to a much greater extent than the centrally planned economies of the East have been integrated by their planners."[2]

The basic reason for the lack of economic integration in Comecon seems to stem from the Marxist policy of disregarding market forces, price mechanisms, and competition, which all lead to a neglect of the benefits of international division of labor. It is perhaps a latent recognition of these factors which has prompted relatively recent attempts at economic reform in the CMEA countries. Before we turn our attention to that, however, we consider the nature of CMEA attempts towards integration.

TOWARDS INTEGRATION

Serious efforts to make Comecon a supranational organization were not exerted until 1962 in the form of proposals to the CMEA by Nikita Khrushchev; those proposals were temporarily discarded when they were flatly rejected by Romania in 1964.[3] Certainly the most important form of intra-CMEA cooperation has so far been the mutual expansion of regional trade. Such expanding trade has grown at a faster pace than individual domestic production, thus increasing the mutual interdependence of the Comecon economies. Nevertheless, efforts towards closer integration have been persistent, and are certainly not limited to the mutual expansion of trade.

The "Fundamental Principles of the International Socialist Division of Labor" of 1962 was accompanied by the Soviets' convincing of the other members of the desirability of a multilateral clearing system, a bloc bank, and a collective bloc currency. By 1966 it was possible to introduce the first coordinated planning of individual five-year plans, and in 1970 the International Investment Bank (IIB) began operations. However, Romania was once again blocking integration attempts, and refused to participate in the IIB. In July 1971, however, a 15- to 20-year integration plan for Comecon was finally announced. In spite of Romania's objections to centralized planning, there has been a definite trend in that direction. Bit by bit, the planning authority of the individual countries seems to be transferring to Comecon, which is slowly but surely assuming more supranational powers. Standardized planning methods and coordination of long-term economic plans have already been established, as well as joint planning offices for individual branches of industry.[4]

The most significant recent development along these lines was the passing by members in July 1971 of the "complex program for the further deepening and streamlining of cooperation and for developing socialist economic integration among the member countries of Comecon." Of note is the fact that this is the first published official document mentioning convertibility as an official aim.[5] Additionally, specialization is supposed to be given far more consideration than in the past, for the 1976-1980 Five-Year Plans, for the first time, will attempt to foster the integration of the individual industries; that is, there will be a gradual phasing out of production that duplicates that of industries in partner countries. More than 20 specialized agencies will operate during this next five-year term to coordinate investment and production in various fields.[6]

The major goals of integration are increased economic growth, a higher standard of living, a higher degree of self-sufficiency for the community, increased defensive strength, and higher and more stable intrabloc trade; the major goal, however, to be achieved over the next 20 years, is the gradual leveling off of the socioeconomic performance levels of the individual members.[7] To facilitate such leveling, the industrially less developed Comecon members are promised preferential treatment and conditions for cooperation. As of now, only Mongolia has been singled out for such preferential treatment, but the program has been viewed as a means of inducing other members, notably Romania, to cooperate more closely with Comecon.[8]

There can be no doubt that intrabloc cooperation has expanded from what was once only mutual trade to areas of joint integration through the coordination of investment plans, specialization, joint undertakings and financial, scientific and technical cooperation. It is the economic planning which makes the Comecon efforts unique, particularly since the mid-1950s, when the autarkic policies were gradually being replaced by various forms of specialization. A special role is played by the International Bank for Economic Cooperation (IBEC), which not only extends economic aid to members at low interest rates, but also, in some cases, allows for trade surpluses with some members to be used to pay for deficits with others.[9]

One key factor in the future integration of Comecon is the dominant role played by the USSR. Increasingly, the smaller members are finding themselves forced to turn to the Soviet Union for assistance, particularly in the area of credits. West German exporters, for example, have come to the conclusion that the limits of East-West trade are being reached, and trade figures tend to bear this out; accordingly, the outcome of the Comecon meeting on the first of July 1975, was more integration instead of less, with trade among the members increasing in the next five years 57 percent over the levels established between 1971-75.[10] In addition to the political and military control from Russia, the economies of the smaller nations have become to a large extent dependent on USSR supplies. In other words, the maneuvering room of the individual Eastern European countries is fairly well restricted.[11]

OBSTACLES TO INTEGRATION

It is now 25 years after the founding of Comecon, and it will be another 20 years, according to CMEA leaders, before the goals of integration can be reached. Accordingly, the obstacles to integration must be fairly great. They are also numerous. Although some of them are certainly surmountable, it appears as if others are not, at least under the present directions of integration. Significantly, the economic factors represent the biggest of stumbling blocks. At any rate, the major impediments of integration are given on the following pages.

National Differences. The "Basic Principles" of the CMEA emphasize national sovereignty, independence, equality, and the need for each country to map out its own development plans according to the concrete conditions in the given country.[12] Two tenets of the Comecon Charter are the principles of interestedness and unanimity, which have been combined to defeat certain actions of the organization. That is, it is possible for a member to declare interest in a particular issue with the intention, through the unanimity requirement, of preventing action by others who are more vitally concerned with the issue. It amounts to the power of veto. Such obstructionist tactics have apparently been made more difficult, however, since the wording has been changed as a result of such tactics to read ". . . council resolution will be adopted only upon agreement of the contracting parties after they have stated their interest in solving a given problem."[13] With regard to specialization, however, it is clear that national differences hinder further integration. East European regimes are not willing to surrender their right to engage in particular branches of industry. Neither are the industrially advanced of them anxious to see new industries established by their more backward neighbors.[14] The U.S. Undersecretary of Political Affairs, Charles Bohlen, has recognized the conflict between nationalism and integration of the Comecon members, and asserts that expanded U.S.-East trade would help to let the CMEA members reassert their national identities, thereby weakening "communist monolithic control."[15] Without doubt, the smaller members of the organization are no longer the pawns they once were. As one author points out, the Soviet Union is still much more equal than the other members, but the smaller members have been able, both individually and collectively, to protect their own national interests on various occasions.[16]

The Question of Supranational Authority. There is obviously a strong element in Comecon, particularly noticeable in the case of Romania, which insists on complete national sovereignty. The Comecon convention in June 1975 saw the Soviet Union, Czechoslovakia, and Bulgaria all urging integration as an end in itself, whereas the Romanian President completely avoided the word "integration" in his speech to the conference and stressed the necessity of individual state actions.[17] Both changing trade patterns and internal economic reform illustrate national objections to supranational authority.

Pricing. The CMEA countries use capitalist world prices in their intrabloc trade, which amounts to an admission of the failure of the CMEA along these lines and produces demoralizing effects. On the other hand, it is recognized that capitalist prices are not a reliable guide to intrabloc specialization and trade, because they do not reflect the conditions of production or exchange under socialism.[18] Such a pricing system makes it impossible for Comecon to evolve its own set of objectively determined prices applicable to blocwide trade. That is, because of the artificial character of the price and wage structures among the member countries, it is impossible to assess, at least rationally, the comparative production costs.[19]

Suspicions of Exploitation. The pricing system used in Comecon, although based on world prices, includes adjustments to counteract cyclical and other market distortions. Thus mark-ups of 50 percent or more are common, so that often the member countries charge each other well above the prices they could obtain in trade with the capitalist countries. This, combined with the inferior quality of the goods, often leads to mutual charges of exploitation, which are particularly strong against the Soviet Union.[20] Countering, the USSR claims that the terms of trade have in fact turned against the Soviets, for the 1966 shift in pricing from the 1957-58 to 1960-64 world averages found the prices of raw materials and fuels being readjusted downward, while the world average of manufactured products increased substantially, a fact which hit the USSR hard in its intrabloc trade.[21] Since then, the Soviet Union found it necessary to raise substantially its price of oil to Comecon members, by 130 percent. This step, taken in January 1975, still leaves the price of oil quite a bit below world prices, but it does represent an effort of the Soviets to improve their terms of trade vis-a-vis CMEA members.[22]

Nonfulfillment of commitments. Ever since World War II, the Comecon nations, because of their overfull employment and because of the nature of their planning, have been plagued with failures to honor undertaken deliveries, faulty specifications, poor quality, and delays. Breaches of this nature have seriously disruptive effects on overall planning and implementation. Sometimes the disruptions are intended, as when it is discovered that hard currencies can be gained from trade with capitalist markets. Thus Czechoslovak machinery, East German precision instruments, Polish coal, and Soviet iron ore have on occasions been diverted to Western countries in spite of previous agreements and acute shortages within the CMEA region.[23]

Declining Role of Intrabloc Trade. As indicated, the CMEA members are increasingly looking to the Western markets. Romania's increased trade with the West, for example, has hurt the CMEA bloc in two ways: it cuts off an outlet for their production due to the bilateral nature of CMEA trade, as well as reduces the total bloc supply of scarce raw materials and foodstuffs.[24] Underlying this, however, is the implicit recognition that CMEA members are simply not satisfied with the present trade patterns.

Complications Through Individual Country Reforms. There can be no question but that the enactment of economic reform programs among the various members of Comecon has vastly complicated integration issues. Although most East European leaders pay lip service to integration, the economic reforms have sent the individual member nations in opposite directions. Accordingly, it will be increasingly difficult to reconcile the patterns into one scheme which would be acceptable to every member. It would seem particularly difficult, for example, to reconcile Hungary's favoring direct and autonomous enterprise-to-enterprise agreements with the Soviet predilection for centralized decision making for an integrated Comecon structure.[25] The feeling among East European commentators is that not only differences in levels of economic development, but also and perhaps more importantly, differences in economic mechanisms or models are eroding any chance of finding common ground upon which to build integration. In practice, almost every country appears to have a different blueprint for Comecon reform.[26]

Structural Differences. There are numerous structural differences among the member countries, and these differences are often extremely large and noticeable. The economic productive potential is distributed quite disproportionately; there are tremendous differences in economic performance levels as measured by overall productivity and living standards; the importance of foreign trade, as mentioned earlier, varies considerably.[27] The growth strategy aimed at the rapid transformation of traditional agrarian or semiagrarian economies has left structural imbalance, and there is an inherent restraint on international resource mobility allowing better allocation.[28]

Integration Methods. As previously indicated, because of the principles on which Comecon is based, it is possible to achieve integration only if such integration does not interfere with the national sovereignty of the states involved. More and more, CMEA efforts have been exerted towards the implementation of middle- and long-term integration; these efforts have mainly stressed structural differences and the development of science and technology. Specific agreements about specialization, which we shall consider shortly, are to be hammered out later. In spite of such efforts, neither the specific areas of coordination nor a method of coordination has been worked out. Because of the "interestedness" clause, coordination can in fact be bilateral or multilateral. As it is working out, the only real achievements have been bilateral in nature, with only insignificant concrete steps having been taken multilaterally.[29]

There are basically five forces which have obstructed efficient plan coordination. First, CMEA-supervised coordination has gone into excessive detail, losing sight of the most important questions of coordinated development. Second, the plans are continually being revised, and individual states are not always willing to accept the revisions. Third, implementation of plans has been particularly unsuccessful for countless reasons. Fourth, the plans are so rigid once set that they do not permit flexible decision making. Finally, the individual countries have not been willing to concentrate on the vital forces of integration, such as investment plans.[30]

CONSIDERATIONS CONCERNING SPECIALIZATION

The division of labor and specialization of production which the complex program envisions are vital to the CMEA if it hopes to achieve any degree of integration. It would not only help achieve more satisfactory growth rates, but would foster intensification of production as well as a reduction in capital absorption. Due to the obstacles to integration which we have already referred to, however, the outlook for successful specialization is not particularly good. Small quantity production, economically unjustified, continues in many phases of Comecon economic life. Identical machine tools are produced in six member countries, electronics in seven, and five members have sugar-processing plants.[31]

The absence of market mechanisms in the bloc makes it extremely difficult to determine patterns of specialization which would be the most economically desirable. Often, mistaken economic policies or objective difficulties hinder the ensuring of economic, technical, infrastructural conditions for utilizing comparative advantages.[32] As we shall see, a minority of the CMEA members even now think that liberalized market conditions are the only method of successful specialization, whereas others are convinced that supranational planning can achieve it. In some cases, such as for primary and extractive industries, specialization is natural and beyond the control of authorities. However, in the manufacturing areas there are countless possibilities, and the Comecon leaders have not as yet even agreed upon the methods of measurement for making unbiased decisions.[33]

Lacking market mechanisms to guide them, comparative advantage somehow has to be determined by the trade officials; accordingly, they have resorted to artificial means, specialization agreements. Two types of international specialization agreements have been used by Comecon. Interproduct specialization allocates the production of a commodity to one or several countries, and is usually found in extractive and primary industries. The other form, that of intraproduct specialization, assigns production according to certain specifications, such as size or model. This type of specialization has assumed particular importance in three major industries: metallurgy, machine building, and chemicals.[34]

Notwithstanding several successful though minor attempts at interproduct specialization, this form is basically stifled by the attitudes of the several Comecon members, as well as the inherent inability to estimate relative cost differences accurately, particularly in the manufactured products. In addition, assignment of production to a less-developed country implied higher costs and was opposed by the other members accordingly. As a result, increasing emphasis has been placed on intraproduct specialization. Since 1964, however, such intraproduct agreements have been fostered through bilateral rather than multilateral cooperation, which in a sense defeats the overall purpose of the scheme.[35]

In addition to these difficulties, many such agreements are never carried out. One well-publicized case, for instance, found Romania allocating the entire output of four-ton trucks to her own market instead of exchanging these, as agreed, for trucks of different models from her partners. Indeed, national self-interest has often hampered successful implementation of plans which otherwise are assumably advantageous in the long run. [36]

One conflict in particular has hindered efforts toward specialization, and that is the conflict between internal industrial development and a rational international division of labor. Despite intense efforts by the Economic Commission of the CMEA, this conflict has not been resolved. However, leveling, one of the aims of the Comecon organization, has seen some success. Industrial growth has proceeded more rapidly in the less-developed member countries than in the more industrialized, as indicated in Table 2.1. Such changes have taken place in spite of the objections of Czechoslovakia, East Germany, and Poland, which needed the markets in the less developed member countries to improve their scales of efficiency and to secure scarce raw materials. In other words, the leveling of industrial production among the members has been at the expense of the more advanced ones. Increasingly, the lack of diversification is having ill effects on the economy of the region as a whole, and CMEA's commitment to balanced development in each of the states has come in conflict with its efforts to achieve a higher degree of specialization. [37]

Still, the major problem seems to be one of measuring relative cost differentials and the lack of an adequate price system to do so. Insulated from outside factors and market mechanisms, imports and exports are determined in accordance with priorities of domestic planning. Additionally, there is a deep-felt need for an index that estimates trade efficiency under dynamic conditions. That is, due to industrial growth, complications arise when one tries to establish each country's comparative advantage. Long-term plans are not well suited to economies which are undergoing rapid structural changes. [38]

The problem is further aggravated by the discrepancies in retail prices among the bloc economies, which remain distorted due to turnover taxes used by all members. The retail prices give no indication whatsoever of consumer demand and preferences, and are useless in the determination of the relative efficiency of consumer goods. [39]

In view of the many obstacles to specialization, there are still only two basic viewpoints as to why specialization has not progressed more rapidly among the Comecon nations. The first centers around the use of world prices in intrabloc trade, whereas the second focuses on the bilateral nature of intrabloc trade. Even should these problems

TABLE 2.1

Changes in Per Capita Income of CMEA Members, 1950 and 1965
(Poland = 100 percent)

	1950	1965
Romania	48	82
Bulgaria	53	83
Soviet Union	82	115
Poland	100	100
Hungary	104	100
East Germany*	115	165
Czechoslovakia	151	144

*East Germany's per capita income was influenced by the population drain between 1950 and 1963.

Source: Stanley Zemelka, "The Problem of Specialization in Comecon," East Europe 18 (May 1969): 11.

be overcome, and there is slight chance of that in the foreseeable future, problems remain. Romanian economists, for instance, reject the theory of specialization according to comparative advantage even in cases where it leads to greater output and consumption for both partners, if the specialization tends to widen the disparity in development levels between the two countries.[40]

CHANCES OF FURTHER INTEGRATION

So far, much more has been said than done about intrabloc specialization. Individual efforts have been taken, and separate arrangements have been made, but these are basically inconsequential. What has been lacking is a system of long-range planning which coordinates the industries of all member countries, instead of the piecemeal projects that have been undertaken. Not only have no long-range plans actually been undertaken towards a more than superficial integration, but, as indicated, there is as yet no agreement on the goals of long-term integration. That is, the members are not in agreement either as to the methods of integration or the aims of integration. In addition to all the hindrances which we already have mentioned is the fact that the individual Comecon members are not in any position to estimate, even approximately, the prospective gains or losses that integration would bring. In spite of general concurrence that it would result in increased prosperity, there exists at present no clear methodical approach to quantify those effects.[41]

Practical considerations have lessened the initial enthusiasm over prospective integration. Indeed, Czechoslovakia and, in particular, Romania, have publicly shown an attitude of skepticism toward the trends developing within Comecon. Hungary and Poland are slowly but surely lining up in their camp, while only Bulgaria and East Germany of the smaller members have continued in their strong orientation toward the idea of a closely knit integration of the CMEA bloc.[42] The openness of the criticism, rare for the Soviet bloc, is a sure sign of the intensity of the differences.

Seen in its proper perspective, the failure of Comecon to integrate on the basis of specialization and intrabloc division of labor cannot be attributed to imperfections in the organization itself, but rather, and more seriously, to a number of characteristics of the economic models on which the state economies are based. Indeed, as Jozef M. P. van Brabant explains,

> "The future of intra-CMEA cooperation relies not on maintaining bilateralism, but on an extensive revision of the CPE's so that multilateral trade and inter-enterprise cooperation will receive the necessary institutional and economic provisions for effective international cooperation. The prerequisites for a successful integration and economic collaboration, in general, do not call for contractual proclamations of multilateralism and the like, but point instead to the necessary economic changes, which will have to precede common agreements on international legal relations."[43]

In short, an adequate integration of the Comecon bloc is impossible as long as the economic mechanisms do not sufficiently provide for the regional assertion of the categories of commodity, value and money, and of the laws of the market related to these categories.[44] When we consider in addition to this the nationalist tendencies and the pattern of economic development within the bloc, the obstacles to integration on any other than superficial levels seem indeed insurmountable. Furthermore, the Comecon organization is effectively limiting integration of its members with outside economies. When Bulgaria in 1975 opposed any permanent multilateral Balkan organization in preference for bilateral pacts, Western observers felt that the act stemmed from Moscow's desire to prevent a Balkan economic bloc rivaling its own dominance of the area's communist economies.[45]

NOTES

1. Wolfgang Schmitz, "Convertibility, Multilateralism and Freedom: A Concept for Recovery and Prosperity," in Convertibility, Multilateralism and Freedom, ed. Wolfgang Schmitz (New York: Springer, 1972), p. vii.

2. Gottfried Haberler, "Theoretical Reflections on the Trade of Socialist Economies," in International Trade and Central Planning, ed. Alan A. Brown and Egon Neuberger (Los Angeles: University of California, 1968), p. 31.

3. Adolf Hermann, "Can Comecon Integrate?," East Europe 18 (May 1969): 15.

4. Glen Alden Smith, Soviet Foreign Trade: Organization, Operations, and Policy, 1918-1971 (New York: Praeger, 1973), pp. 28, 205.

5. Wolfgang Schmitz, "Monetary Dynamic Forces in East and West: Important Developments in the Seventies," in Convertibility, Multilateralism and Freedom, ed. Wolfgang Schmitz (New York: Springer, 1972), p. 233.

6. "Comecon—The Next Five Years," Business International 22 (March 7, 1975): 76.

7. Heinrich Machowski, "Toward a Socialist Economic Integration of Eastern Europe," in Eastern Europe in the 1970s, ed. Sylva Sinanian, Istvan Deak, and Peter C. Ludz (New York: Praeger, 1972), p. 190.

8. Henry Wilcox Schaefer, Comecon and the Politics of Integration (New York: Praeger, 1972), p. 161.

9. J. Wilczynski, The Economics of Socialism (London: Allen and Unwin, 1970), pp. 195-99.

10. "Comrades Unite," The Economist 256 (July 5, 1975): 123.

11. James R. Basche, Jr., East-West Trade: The Lessons From Experience (New York: Conference Board, 1971), p. 21.

12. Jozef M. P. van Brabant, Essays on Planning in Eastern Europe (Rotterdam: Rotterdam University, 1974), p. 18.

13. Schaefer, op. cit., p. 52.

14. Richard F. Staar, The Communist Regimes in Eastern Europe (Stanford: Stanford University, 1971), pp. 258-59.

15. Maynard P. Venema, "The Rumanian Refinery Project -- The Negotiation, Structure, and Finance of A Major American Corporate Venture in Eastern Europe," in Financing East-West Business

Transactions, ed. American Management Association, Inc. (New York: American Management Association, 1968), p. 36.

16. William R. Kintner and Wolfgang Klaiber, Eastern Europe and European Security (New York: Dunellen, 1971), p. 207.

17. Viktor Meier, "Schwierige Integration im Ostblock," Frankfurter Allgemeine Zeitung, July 16, 1975, p. 9.

18. Wilczynski, op. cit., pp. 200-01.

19. Michael Gamarnikow, "Is Comecon Obsolete?," East Europe 17 (April 1968): 12.

20. Wilczynski, op. cit., p. 201.

21. Gamarnikow, op. cit., p. 14.

22. "Comrades Unite," op. cit., p. 123.

23. Wilczynski, op. cit., p. 202.

24. John Michael Montias, "Economic Nationalism in Eastern Europe: Forty Years of Continuity and Change," in Eastern Europe In Transition, ed. Kurt London (Baltimore: Johns Hopkins, 1966), p. 198.

25. Kintner and Klaiber, op. cit., p. 207.

26. Wolfgang Klaiber, "East-West Trade and U. S. Objectives in Eastern Europe," in East-West Trade and the Technology Gap: A Political and Economic Appraisal, ed. Stanislaw Wasowski (New York: Praeger, 1970), p. 209.

27. Machowski, op. cit., pp. 190-91.

28. Brabant, op. cit., pp. 24, 120.

29. Machowski, op. cit., p. 192.

30. Brabant, op. cit., pp. 33-34.

31. Stanley Zemelka, "The Problem of Specialization in Comecon," East Europe 18 (May 1969): 9.

32. Sandor Ausch, Theory and Practice of CMEA Cooperation (Budapest: Akademiai Kiado, 1972), p. 215.

33. Gamarnikow, op. cit., p. 16.

34. Zemelka, op. cit., p. 10.

35. Ibid.

36. Ibid.

37. Ibid., p. 11.

38. Ibid., p. 12.

39. Ibid.

40. Montias, op. cit., pp. 198-99.

41. Machowski, op. cit., p. 197.

42. Samuel Pisar, Coexistence and Commerce (New York: McGraw-Hill, 1970), p. 16.

43. Jozef M. P. van Brabant, Bilateralism and Structural Bilateralism in Intra-CMEA Trade (Rotterdam: Rotterdam University, 1973), pp. 17-19.

44. Ausch, op. cit., p. 226.

45. Richard F. Janssen, "Balkans Forge Closer Economic Ties," Wall Street Journal, June 7, 1976, p. 4.

CHAPTER 3

ECONOMIC REFORM WITHIN COMECON

We have discovered a basic dilemma in our discussion of the integration of Comecon nations. On the one hand, we have ascertained that any long-term, other than superficial integration must be preceded by basic and far-reaching economic reforms among the nations concerned. On the other hand, we have also indicated that economic reform, as it is now being implemented, is one of the obstacles to further integration. Accordingly, it would be advantageous to look more closely at the economic reforms which have been, and are being, undertaken. First, we shall consider the individual reform programs separately; then we shall try to determine if there is, in fact, a reform program which is regionwide.

BULGARIA

As previously indicated, Bulgaria is one of the closest adherents to the policies of the USSR.[1] This is reflected in the directions of her economic reforms. Directions, because Bulgaria has had not one, but two blueprints for economic reform. A pre-1968 blueprint, without openly renouncing central planning and management, had been forward-looking in spirit and had included many liberalizing changes similar to those of other Comecon members. However, the plan was never implemented. The 1968 plan was a reversal of such tendencies. Centralized planning was expanded rather than narrowed; complusory indexes were increased rather than reduced; market forces were stifled rather than welcomed. All in all, Bulgaria returned in 1968 to the harsh guidelines of the Stalin era (though certainly not to the same extent as Albania).

The official rationale for the 1968 model is the necessity of taking advantage of the "scientific-technical revolution," which hardly seems feasible in the light of the fact that Bulgaria is one of the technologically backward members of Comecon. Objective observers from the outside find it much more plausible to explain the reversal in terms of the reluctance of the regime to take steps which might endanger the tight grip of the party over the Bulgarian society. In addition, others argue that such a backward economy can much better afford central planning and a command economy than can an industrially developed society. This appears to be questionable, in view of the fact that, whereas the costs and burdens of centralization are perhaps less obvious in a less-developed country, they are nevertheless real and present. The case of Yugoslavia, incidentally, seems to belie the assumed inverse correlation between level of development and necessity of command.

Our review of the economic situation in which Bulgaria finds herself indicates that there are good reasons for reform. Consequently, it would be advantageous to consider what the pre-1968 plan envisioned. Her problems were typical of a Soviet type command economy, such as excessive centralization and planning; the stifling of efficiency; deficiency of motivation and incentives; arbitrary price formation; and general inadequacy of measurement criteria.

Actually, the role of central planning was never questioned by the Bulgarian leadership: extensive decentralization was never considered. However, attempts were made to reshuffle the chain of command so that the enterprises themselves appeared to have more authority. The enterprises were charged with becoming profitable operations, but the freedom they were given to do this extended only to insignificant details. Efforts were made toward internal financing of the enterprises in place of the former state allocations, but in fact most investment projects were to remain centrally determined, and the state maintained its financing of investments in all priority sectors, especially in heavy industry where most of the unprofitable enterprises were to be found.

An attempt was made to tie wages and salaries to the profitability of the enterprises; this resulted only in a chaotic situation which had to be scrapped immediately. Revisions in the tax system were also designed to stimulate profitability, but they instead acted to dampen incentive. The novel feature was a progressive income profits tax on enterprises, which had the contradictory aims of promoting incentive and at the same time discouraging undue increases in wages and profits. A revision of the pricing system was attempted, but so many exceptions and alterations were necessary that in the long run, the old price system remained virtually unchanged. The reforms barely touched the vital section of foreign trade except for an announced revision of customs duties, possible future contracts between the Bulgarian authorities and foreign enterprises, and repeated pleas to producers to make exports more profitable.

As a consequence of these failures, a recentralization instead of decentralization took place in 1968. However, concentrated attention was given to revisions of price lists, and price reform became a central issue. Although the moves indicated the desire of the government to come to terms with the pricing system and to rationalize the price structure, there was no sign of any intent to permit market forces to determine prices of even a limited number of consumer goods.

Finally, the Planning Decree of 1970 took a further step backwards, even making some of the liberalized remnants of the 1968 reversal obsolete, such as those pertaining to greater reliance on internal financing and bank loans instead of government allocations of capital. In the area of foreign trade, there has been an additional restriction on direct dealings between Bulgarian economic trusts and foreign enterprises, reversing the liberalized outlook of just a few years earlier. Such measures were taken in part due to "gross violations of financial discipline" by the merchant fleet supertrust, and have made clear that no real autonomy is permitted below the Foreign Trade Ministry. (In a later move, foreign trade enterprises were made subsidiaries of state economic associations, and are no longer part of the Ministry of Foreign Trade.)[2]

Thus the attempts at reform were both short-lived and unfruitful. Besides the many economic reasons for the failure, one reason was all too obvious: managerial incompetence. Not only was it difficult to change the skill and mentality of the managers, but they were alarmingly poorly educated to begin with. Functioning as supervisors with little need for initiative or decision making, they were unable to adjust to the disciplines of true management.[3]

In addition, Bulgaria was plagued with all sorts of other problems. The economics of industrial location had been neglected in Bulgarian planning, with 53 percent of industrial production concentrated in nine cities, which resulted in regional imbalance. Bulgaria had reached the lowest level ever of its population growth, which reduced the most productive factor in her economy. Warehouses became crammed with unwanted goods to such an extent that desired goods could be purchased by consumers only if they agreed to buy also an unwanted good. Machinery representing millions of dollars remained unpacked for years because no one realized it was available.

Some enterprises had stockpiles of raw materials that would last at least 30 years. Productivity remained exceedingly low due to improper staffing, with managers appointed politically and engineers working as manual laborers. Finally, those enterprises given most credit for achievement were often far from the most efficient.[4] The reform experiment lasted only two years, hardly time enough to correct the many problems, and certainly not enough time to assess accurately the results of the experiment.

Generally, Bulgaria has followed the lines of the Soviet-type reform, and is the only East European country not to have found itself in the slightest conflict with that line. Additionally, the invasion of Czechoslovakia found her drawing even closer to that line. Accordingly, observers foresee no major advance in the reform effort on the part of Bulgaria until and unless the Soviet Union leads the way.[5] The reasons for reform, however, are persistent and more than apparent.

CZECHOSLOVAKIA

It was Czechoslovakia which, before 1950 even, was the first to try to combine the market with national economic planning.[6] This was a two-year macroeconomic experiment quite different from the Soviet-type plan applied later on, and was suppressed on the pretext of the cold war, although most sources explain the suppression in terms of the reform's variance from the policies of the USSR. A second attempt at reform occurred in 1957-58, and focused on reorganization of planning and management to improve efficiency. When the Third Five-Year Plan broke down, however, officials found the cause to be the decentralization process (in spite of evidence to the contrary), and reversed the tendencies. By 1963, the economy had broken down, with total production and national income declining even in absolute terms.

That breakdown led to new reform efforts, which again concentrated on the introduction of market forces. The disastrous economic situation at the time allowed the reformers to assert themselves. Besides changing the central management apparatus, the plan sought to change the function of prices and of foreign trade. The conclusion was reached that economic prices should be introduced, that is, prices which could develop only in a real market and under the pressure of competition. This was done by the introduction of three price groups, which was necessary to avoid inflationary tendencies: a first group centrally fixed as before, a second group of "limit prices" allowed to fluctuate within prescribed limits, and a third group of free prices.

A price reform failed in 1966 because it was intentionally sabotaged by the affected ministries, and because prices were pushed up by the enterprises under the pretext of high costs, which led to excessive profits. Therefore, the desired economic pressure failed to materialize, with the result not one of efficiency, but of inflation. This unsuccessful price reform later was used as an argument against reforms in general.

An attempt was made also to rationalize foreign trade by decentralization and by making such trade more competitive by basing it on profit criteria. This attempt, like that of pricing, was abandoned in 1968, along with any thoughts of decentralization. Producers no longer have freedom of choice in foreign trade, and compulsory targets have been reintroduced. As in the case of Bulgaria, much of the problem of reform lies in the fact that the political system uses personal-power criteria to fill the key positions not only in government, but in industry. Loyalty, not ability, is the deciding factor.

The extent of reform envisioned by its architects is indicated by its goals: switching from an extensive economy dominated by centrally prescribed quantitative targets to a more autonomous intensive economy stressing qualitative factors; replacing the seller's market with a genuine buyer's market; and exposing producers to the pressures of a truly competitive market mechanism. Individual enterprises were to earn their own way. Not only were investments to be financed by enterprises from their own resources or by borrowing with interest payments, but profits, as realized by sales rather than by fulfillment of planned production targets, were to be the main criterion of economic efficiency.[7]

The reversal came in 1969 when, under new leadership, the state returned to central planning and abandoned the "romantic notions about the omnipotence of the market."[8] As in the case of Bulgaria, the result was a step backward towards Stalinist restoration. Such is not surprising when we note the close interrelatedness of economic and political reform. Actually, the economic reformers had come to the conclusion that a reform of the political system had to go hand in hand with the economic reform, and that democratism was an indispensable condition of the effective functioning of modern economies.[9] The invasion of the armies of five Warsaw Pact countries put an end to such thoughts, at least temporarily. Since the invasion Czechoslovakia, once a strong ally of the reformers on many CMEA issues, is more than ever firmly entrenched in the Soviet camp, at least officially.[10] Demoralization has brought such ideas of progress to a virtual standstill.

It is unlikely that any major reforms will be introduced in the 1976-80 plan. The problems, however, are growing worse. Besides those in the energy field, the major challenges include chronic labor shortages, aging plants and equipment, a declining domestic raw materials base, overly cautious managers, lack of initiative, and scarcity of hard currency with which to buy essential imports. Those problems are not new, but the urgency is, for the government must fulfill both the rising demands of domestic consumption as well as the demands of production commitments, primarily with other CMEA countries.[11]

GERMAN DEMOCRATIC REPUBLIC

For all practical purposes, East Germany has been under a command economy since the First World War.[12] Though it took different forms, all had the following in common: central economic management according to political considerations, a weakening of the market mechanism, stable prices, and similar administrative procedures in allocating both capital and manpower. Thus the "socialist revolution" was simply a supplement rather than a replacement of the existing economic order.

A number of factors after World War II theoretically should have encouraged intensive economic growth: the shortage of labor, the favorable industrial structure, the highly developed skills of the population, the pragmatic economic policy, and the relatively high level of technology. However, the capital-output ratio grew extremely fast, and confirmed that a decline of investment effectiveness and overall capital efficiency was taking place. For this reason, an economic reform was instigated in 1963.

Some major features of the reform plan were a reduction in the number of plan targets, an increased role of profit as a criterion of enterprise effectiveness, increased authority for enterprises in the areas of sales and supplies, rights to select enterprises to conduct export transactions, and decentralization in the formation of the plan. Although these steps sound similar to the steps taken in other Comecon nations, they were in fact different. The decentralization of decision making, for instance, did not result in the enterprises gaining authority, but rather technocrats who, like the bureaucrats, worked for the government. Also, the price reform took place at wholesale levels, which ignored supply-and-demand relationships, lowering the ability of the management to regulate the structural changes that were called for in production programs. The technocratic reform, while it sounds good, strives for nothing more than an adjustment of the command system to the economic determinants of an industrially advanced country, rather than the replacement by market considerations.

It is not surprising that reform in the German Democratic Republic has taken on different forms than in the other Comecon nations, for East Germany, unlike the others, has not faced economic stagnation and constant economic crises. Instead of trying to go into that in detail, let it only be noted that economic reform in East Germany has been more political than economic, while the reverse is true in the other CMEA states. In fact, East Germany has a more rigid ideological regime than any other Comecon nation, including the Soviet Union.

As far as economic reform concerns foreign trade directly, there has been an extension of direct participation of producing enterprises in foreign trade transactions. The reform follows three patterns: specialized foreign trade enterprises are set up for sectoral industrial associations; direct foreign trade rights are granted to large production units; and combined domestic and foreign trading enterprises are established in various sectors.[13]

Actually, economic reform in East Germany is not literally reform. The aim of it is to make the economic system more efficient, but without abolishing its essential elements. Profit and prices are here the main keys, and as long as they are centrally determined, there will remain the inherent conflicts and shortcomings which earmark CMEA as a whole.[14]

HUNGARY

Hungary is the sole member of Comecon which has so far adopted the system of regulated and planned market economy.[15] In light of this, it would be advantageous to consider its problems before the reform. Conflicts and inefficiency had arisen due to a number of problems: the pace and extent of forced industrialization; exaggerated emphasis on heavy industry; the policy of autarky, with its tendency to create industries for which Hungary lacked raw materials, skilled management, and labor; blind imitation of the Soviet economic model, which misfit the country; excessive rate of investment at the expense of consumption. These are found, to varying degrees, in all CMEA small members. The balance had become misbalanced. Neglect of the agricultural sector had created an acute shortage of export goods, resulting in a shortage of hard currency. The neglect of consumer goods led to stagnation and to a decline in the standard of living. Generally, there was capital waste and low efficiency due to the establishment of uncompetitive, high-cost, low-productivity industries.

The reform was put into effect on January 1, 1968, all at once, unlike other reforms which have attempted to gradually introduce changes. Only in such a way, the reformers reasoned, could the evils of central planning be done away with. A central plan did, of course, continue to establish the main objectives of the national economy, and to determine the allocation of resources to realize those objectives. The plan then is not simply a synthesis of plan and market, but of a regulated market, regulated not only by economic instruments, but partly also by administrative instruments. Actually, the Hungarian market reform is a synthesis of the unity of state ownership with the autonomy of economic units.[16]

Basically, there are seven economic regulators replacing the former plan targets. The first is a price policy aimed at stabilizing the retail prices of basic commodities. Only the prices of the most important raw materials are centrally fixed: others are centrally limited, and a large number of prices are determined by agreement between buyers and sellers. The second regulator regards the development of personal incomes: only aggregates are determined by central authorities, with the enterprises free to adjust wages and salaries as they see fit. The third regulator concerns investment policy, with enterprise investment steadily gaining prevalence over state investment. Fourth, there have been established three types of credit (short-, medium-, and long-term), with only long-term credits under close supervision of the state. The fifth regulator is that of foreign trade, closely linked to central planning because the state has a number of commitments which must be fulfilled by the enterprises. Finally, there are fiscal and budgetary regulators which directly affect the enterprises.[17]

Although the Hungarian reform goes beyond all other Comecon reforms in its relationship to market mechanisms, it stops short of a genuine market reform, since it can operate freely only as long as it does not conflict with the objectives and priorities of the state planners. Still, it has been fairly successful in establishing economic factors, such as profit, loss, and wage incentives, in the place of the highly centralized, rigid system of the past. Accordingly, the enterprises have gained a considerable degree of authority over their own operations, especially in such matters as what they produce, how much they charge, and what they do with their profits, as well as, in the cases of the larger concerns, dealing for themselves in foreign trade. That is, the central plan is merely an indicative guideline rather than an absolute directive. The enterprises thus make their own contributions to the planning process, making it more realistic, while greater reliance is placed on indirect control of the economy by the state through financial and monetary policies.[18]

By 1970, some results were apparent. Besides ensuring a continued rise in living standard, production, and trade, the consequences were an increase in the effect of demand on production and a corresponding increase in the variety of goods available; a revision of the entire production structure, and thus of the system of supply; sales had increased faster than production, thus reducing the rate of stockpiling; the foreign trade balance, for the first time in many years, was positive with both East and West; and for the first time, the rate of growth of agricultural production exceeded that of industry. In addition, the transition had been smoother than anticipated. Difficulties persisted, however, particularly in regard to prices, subsidies, and turnover tax systems.

In regard to foreign trade, the Hungarian planners realized that an overly hasty release of trade from administrative control could cause pressures resulting from domestic shortages that would have an adverse effect on the balance of payments. Accordingly, many restrictions have been retained, such as foreign exchange controls, quotas, foreign trade permits, and import deposits. Of deciding influence, however, is the spirit in which these restrictions are used: they could be used as protective measures, simply favoring those sections of the economy which are not sufficiently internationally competitive, or they could be used to stimulate domestic efficiency by increasing the pressure of foreign competition. So far, indications are that Hungarian trade policy is departing from its former, strictly bilateral patterns and is becoming more flexible and more alert to comparative cost advantages.[19]

Certainly the Hungarian reform is no assurance of the development of a relatively free market system, although increasingly, the enterprise decisions will be made on the basis of market factors. Primarily, the enterprises have won the authority to make short-term plans, whereas all long-term planning will continue to be a function of the state. For that reason, it has been maintained that the Hungarian reform is not an economic reform, but a managerial one.[20] There have been, however, no indications of a retreat from the principles of the new economic mechanism, and we would prefer to consider it as indeed a true economic reform. Significantly, the central planning of the command type has changed not merely in detail, but in principle, and that the enterprises have true decision-making autonomy, which is quite different from the illusion of enterprise freedom in the other CMEA countries, is a consideration which should not be ignored.

POLAND

Poland, since 1957, has made three abortive attempts to introduce three qualitatively different economic reforms. Each time, the plans had to be abandoned either because of sabotage by the party establishment or due to acute economic crises. Lack of a coherent policy and absence of consistent leadership have combined with inner party struggles to effectively handicap all reform efforts.[21]

The 1957 reform plan had envisioned drastic decentralization, autonomy of the individual enterprise, and the increasing influence of market forces, such as prices reflecting the costs of production and the mechanisms of supply and demand. Both the internal and external (CMEA) environments, politically, were not ripe for such drastic changes. By mid-1959, all political leaders associated with the reform program had been ousted from positions of authority.[22]

By 1963, due to serious economic difficulties, the ruling elite showed renewed interest in reform. Again, emphasis was placed on decentralization of decision making, profitability and cost accounting as the measures of efficiency, and a plan of careful market research. However, the blueprint for reform contained so many safeguards that it neutralized the positive aspects of the program. In contrast to the first reform, this was sponsored not by the liberals, but by the middle-of-the-roaders, under the pressure of economic necessity. This second reform resulted in very little structural change, and was based not on theoretical rationale, but simply on expediency. As it turned out, the direction of the reform seemed advantageous, but it was not implemented due to the sabatoge of dogmatists and hardliners.[23]

By 1968, the economic situation had not changed. There was a huge overcommitment of scarce capital goods; investment cycles dragged on for years; employment was well above planned targets; low labor productivity persisted; and there was a drastic disparity between product mix and effective industrial and consumer demand. Using 1969-70 as a transitory period, the party announced a new reform for the coming Five-Year Plan (1971-75). First, the direction of the planning process was to be reversed, with planning to be built from the bottom upwards, with the enterprises establishing their own goals. Actually, this was not a true step toward decentralization, however, since the plans were to be approved by the central planners, who also still had complete control of long-term planning. It simply put some of the planning burden, rather than responsibility, on the enterprises. The other two key features of the reform plan involved investment financing and an ill-fated system of material incentives. Instead of state allocation of free investment grants, a new system of interest-bearing loans (3 percent) was arranged. This resulted in no favorable change at all, however, for it was still the state which had to decide among the many claims for the limited investment funds. The incentive program failed not because it was a bad idea, but because there was no method of objectively determining efficiency levels.[24]

In considering the reasons for the failures of the Polish reforms, two factors should be considered: the quality of the blueprints for reform and the policy of its implementation. In the case of Poland, both factors worked to undermine the reforms. The economic crises of Poland had put pressure on the planners. Without pressure, no far-reaching reform would be initiated; but with pressure, the reforms must be initiated without thorough detailed analysis. There have been five groups of irreconcilable policies which are mainly responsible for the failure of the Polish reforms. First is the simultaneous use of administrative orders and economic parameters, similar to the cases of East German and Bulgaria, which often results in conflict. Second is the preservation of the basic features of the traditional economic system while trying to change enterprise behavior, although the first is a determinant of the second. Third is the simultaneous use of yearly planning targets and long-term financial norms: in Polish industry the practice of changing financial norms several times a year is almost universal. Fourth is simultaneous decentralization at enterprise and branch level, which undermines the authority of those who have responsibility. Fifth is the preservation of taut planning with simultaneous changes in management mechanism: effective economic reforms and very taut planning simply cannot be reconciled. We have already referred to the hesitancy of the apparatus to implement the reforms. In addition, there were serious obstacles due to the piecemeal implementation during the transition periods.[25]

Still, Poland is bit by bit pursuing its hectic course of reform, aimed now primarily at decentralization of authority in the industrial sphere. Since January 1, 1973, some 30 major industries have been reconstituted as "large economic organizations," whose managers exercise greater control over wages, employment, plant organization, investment policy, and even foreign trade. The managers are still unable, however, to set prices or adjust product mix. Even should the trend towards decentralization continue, there is no indication that economic reform will lead to an increased reliance on market forces rather than on central planning to determine the allocation of resources.[26]

ROMANIA

Romania has taken the conservative road to reform. Aimed at more effective planning and control, its blueprints for reform make no attempt to combine elements of the market mechanism with the socialist economy. The measures, designed to rationalize and increase economic effectiveness instead of to decentralize, might lead to systematic improvements, but no solution to the problems inherent in central planning. Still, the plans call for an avoidance of excessive centralism and for greater management responsiblity and economic efficiency. Such convervatism seems incongruent with Romania's rather independent foreign policy, which has plagued CMEA for two decades.[27]

It is primarily due to political factors that Romania has introduced no actual economic reforms, although insistence on centralism has been explained by the fact that the country is only now going through its period of industrialization. In addition, there is an acute shortage of qualified managers at the lower levels. Both of these arguments seem to be more excuse than reason. Romania's position vis-a-vis to the USSR seems to be of prime importance, for its independence in foreign policy depends in part on the stability of its economic system. Marketization at this time would create internal disturbances which would threaten national unity and thus weaken the country's leadership vis-a-vis the other Comecon nations. Furthermore, a technocratic reform such as that of East Germany is impossible due to the country's lack of qualified experts.[28]

Romania, certainly one of the least industrialized countries when the CMEA was formed, has made remarkable strides in her all-out effort to industrialize. That was, in fact, the major conflict with the USSR, which wanted Romania to implement the principle of the socialist division of labor by concentrating on areas other than heavy industry.[29] Besides political problems, the industrialization program has led to other problems too. There has been a serious imbalance in overall growth, which threatens further economic development even more directly than the persistent low quality of goods, inadequate services, and apathetic workers. Inflexibility in planning and implementation is becoming less and less appropriate for Romania's stage of development, which is reflected in the ever increasing bottlenecks and shortages.[30]

In regard to foreign trade, Romania's position is steadily worsening, and its per capita external trade is lower than that of other small CMEA members. Due to an increasingly unfavorable balance-of-payments position, foreign trade reform was forthcoming in March 1971, when foreign investors were finally afforded the opportunity to hold up to 49 percent equity of a joint-owned company. Also, the monopoly of the Ministry of Foreign Trade was broken, and industrial ministries took over many of the foreign trade functions. Finally, new rules on foreign currency allowances were devised, with each industrial ministry being given targets for debits and credits. In all aspects, the state remains in charge of planning and implementation, in spite of the talk of "reform."[31] If, in fact, Romanian foreign trade policies can be considered as "liberalized," then there is little correlation between these and their domestic counterpart. The same can be said for Romanian foreign policy in general, which has been described as white on the outside and red on the inside.[32]

PROSPECTS FOR CMEA-WIDE REFORM

In considering the possibility of CMEA-wide reform, the individual reform patterns which have just been reviewed should be kept in mind. For now, we shall look into the causes of reform in the CMEA, the steps taken, the impediments to region-wide reform, and the prospects of meaningful reform within the bloc as a whole.

Causes of Reform

It is obvious that each of the countries under consideration has found it necessary to introduce economic reforms of some type, although the blueprints have in each case been different, and the implementation successful to widely differing degrees. At the heart of each reform, however, lies the same thing: inadequate previous economic performance. Accordingly, it would be advantageous to consider the underlying causes which prompted the reforms in the first place. Basically, the problems which made the reforms necessary fall in two groups: those related to central planning in general, and those related to the particular stage of economic development in which the countries found themselves.

Most of the defects of central planning are obvious. There is a communication problem both upwards and downwards, and the upwards screening process is often far from objective; at any rate, the information on which decisions are made is always distorted or incomplete, whether by intent or not. In the other direction, plan implementation is seldom as anticipated, for hundreds of reasons. In addition, the planners have seldom anticipated the preferences of consumers, so that shortages and surpluses are a constant problem. Furthermore, central planning has created a class of managers not really qualified to manage. Overambitious planning and central allocation of resources have led to a sellers' market which promotes hoarding, a deterioration of product quality, constant delays, and inefficient use of capital.

Centrally determined prices have led to a multitude of other problems.[33]

Stalin's legacy of centrally controlled economies and forced industrialization has proved to be not readily adaptable to the demands of an increasingly complex economy. In fact, the major objective of reform has been to overcome the inefficiencies created in the first years of the industrialization processes.[34] Due not only to causes rooted in the individual economies, but also to the overall inadequacy of CMEA specialization and cooperation, are insufficiency of raw materials available for export, overproduction of goods produced in parallel, low technological levels, low efficiency, and shortage of products which have attained world quality standards. Advocates of closer CMEA integration maintain that these problems are directly due to the bilateral nature of CMEA coordination, and that disproportions rose on the entire regional level which were unforeseen in the relations between any two given nations.[35]

Another explanation of planning difficulties is found in the scale of such planning. When the goals were few and immediate, as when CMEA was founded, a rechanneling of resources was possible, such as from the agricultural sector to that of heavy industry. When the priority sectors increased in number however, such as when agriculture, residential construction, and consumer demands could no longer be neglected, serious bottlenecks resulted. Also, collective consumption and rising standards of living create the sine qua non for a continuous rise in labor productivity.[36] It has been stated elsewhere that planned economies are somewhat more effective in mobilizing resources than they are efficient in using them.[37]

Other inherent shortcomings in CMEA planning have been the lack of economic motivation, the absence of a basis for exact economic accounting, the dominance of political and ideological rather than economic considerations in decision making, misallocation of decision-making responsibility, and insufficient incentives to technological progress.[38] Still, the early autarkic policies were perhaps the most glaring mistakes, which led to deformities of the regional economy, disintegration of national macroeconomics, and inefficiency of national microeconomics. In the early period, for example, large steel factories were built in East Germany, Poland, Czechoslovakia, Hungary and Bulgaria, but none of these countries had either the access to resources or market necessary for such an industry.[39]

As far as the stage of development is concerned, reform has been fostered by the realization among the Comecon nations that they are ending the period of acute shortages and entering into a new and more balanced phase where the objective consists in the satisfaction of needs on a higher plane; accordingly, the planned economy needs more flexible methods.[40] Not only did the elimination of basic scarcities make changes in the economic system inevitable, but also the opening of trade routes to the West, which necessitated new trading institutions and production priorities.[41]

Basically, however, it was the end of the extensive growth period which necessitated economic reform. The transition period, marked by a devastating increase in capital-output ratio, was one in which increments in output by raising net investments were simply no longer feasible. Qualitative improvement of labor and capital was necessary to make up for the slower quantitative increase, and during the 1960s increased efficiency became recognized as the central target in the economic reforms.[42]

Reform Measures Taken

There are essentially two alternatives for a reform of a command economy. The first is marketization, in which the nonmarket economy is transformed into market economy, command planning is replaced by indicative planning, and centralized decision making is decentralized. The second, technocratization, does not change the command basis, but merely the criteria of decision making and the forms of management: its main aim is to limit the influence of ideological and political factors in economic decision making wherever they prevent a rational, economically justified, feasible solution. The reforms so far undertaken show a wide range within these two extremes. The Czechoslovak reform of 1968, which was immediately suppressed, came closest to the marketization reform, while the East German reform has been closest to the technocratic reform model. Still, all systems have been somewhat decentralized, and the decision making base expanded.[43]

There are a number of reform measures taken which are common to all countries under consideration. Planning is less prescriptive and less detailed, and there is a shift in emphasis from short-term to long-term planning. There is a greater independence of the enterprises. Profit has been accepted as a main indicator of performance. Material incentives to labor have been strengthened. Varying degrees of price reform have been achieved. There is a greater role assigned to finance and credit. A closer link between production and distribution has been realized. Finally, all countries have shown a stronger orientation to foreign trade, and a lessening of the former autarkic tendencies.[44] The fact that these reforms have taken place in each of the countries, although to be sure in different degrees, should not be surprising. First, we had earlier indicated that the problems of these countries show many similarities. Second, however, is the fact that reforms in one communist country generate pressures for similar changes in the others.[45]

Impediments to CMEA-Wide Reform

In spite of similar problems, mutual influences, and common efforts, there are many and serious impediments to CMEA-wide reform. We have noted earlier that each Comecon nation seems to have a different blueprint for reform, and that these are based primarily on national priorities. The Romanians favor bilateralism; the Hungarians, Czechoslovaks, and Poles are not opposed to multilateralism, but insist on currency convertibility as a prerequisite for it; the East Germans oppose this demand, whereas the Soviets have been more or less ambivalent on the issue. Another conflict arises from the fact that the Hungarians and Czechoslovaks wish to decentralize Comecon so that enterprises could deal directly with each other, whereas the East Germans and Soviets advocate stronger centralization not only domestically, but also for Comecon.[46]

True, there are factors, both economic and political, which lessen the impact of such disagreements. Romania, for instance, has long fought against the idea of a supranational organization, but again and again is forced to concede. Thus Romania refused to join the Intermetall organization when it was set up in 1964, but began cooperating with it in 1970. In May 1970, Romania refused to join the newly created Investment Bank of Comecon, but became a member in February of the next year. Likewise, it joined Interchim, another Comecon organization, in late 1970, a year after all other members of the CMEA had joined. In each case, economic and political pressures forced the about face.[47]

Still, there are other obstacles. Romanian economists, for instance, maintain that the transferral of national planning techniques to supranational levels is simply not feasible.[48] In addition to that, all political leaders in the smaller Comecon states inherently react against reforms which would tend, in the long run, to weaken their power positions:[49] this could be either through decentralization at home or centralization on the Comecon level.

Prospects for CMEA-Wide Reform

One of the basic requirements for reform on the supranational level is that the national economic mechanisms be changed.[50] To the extent that at least two members have shown no intentions of significant national reform, the chances for reform on a higher level are slim. That is, reforms as well as further attempts towards closer integration of the CMEA economies cannot be successful through, for instance, the introduction of regional free trading and monetary convertibility as long as the region is without an economically justified price system and as long as the individual systems retain their non-market, directional control through central planning and artificially fixed prices.[51]

On the other hand, modernization is not a condition, but a process. The individual states must, of necessity, change according to changing conditions. The question then depends on the compatibility of changes in any given nation with those of the others. Then again, the direction of change does not depend on economics alone. If so, marketization and decentralization would occur in each of the countries. Instead, political and social influences have strong bearings on future developments. In short, the introduction of genuine, qualitative economic reforms in communist countries encourages the emergence of pluralistic political tendencies, so that the economic considerations are often subordinate to the power structure.[52] At the same time, the power structure is in jeopardy if reforms are not forthcoming, simply because of the economic crisis which will appear.

Increasingly, the individual nations are questioning not only the separate aspects of CMEA policy, but the idea of integration itself. According to William F. Robinson,

> The bilateral method of clearing accounts . . . ; the lack of a genuinely transferable ruble, let alone a convertible currency; the lack of realistic exchange rates; the failure to establish a modern credit and banking system; the excessive duplication of manufacturing and investments; the distortion of price relationships . . . ; the poor coordination of planning. . . ; the absence of a regional market for goods, capital, and labor; . . . have all been discussed in a growing number of articles in the press and professional journals, and by Party and state officials in their speeches and reports."[53]

Such nationalist feelings expressed in opposition to a supranational structure makes one thing clear: specialization or reform on a supranational level is not necessarily the optimal or desirable condition for the individual member. Accordingly, it is necessary, as previously mentioned, that each individual country undergo its reform before further consideration of reform on a supranational level is taken. That, then, returns us to the question of the individual reform efforts. We have seen that they are piecemeal, and, for the most part, not reforms at all. Instead of a true change in the structure and functional aspects of the economy, they have, in large, simply been efforts to increase efficiency while maintaining control at the top, restrictions on the horizon, and conflicts underneath.

Simply, the structure of Comecon is not suitable for reform. Conceived in the spirit of downward flow, it really has no capabilities for reacting efficiently to decisions that flow upward or from the outside, meaning individual state deviations or the forces of market mechanisms. This latter, inherent conflict with market forces which results from such an approach of centralized planning, even though in the form of de-bureaucratization, is of prime importance as we now consider the twin structural features that lie at the base of the economic systems and which must be considered, in the long run, as the target for any authentic reform of the CMEA: bilateralism and currency inconvertibility.

NOTES

1. Unless otherwise noted, the information in this section has been gleaned from L. A. D. Dellin, "Bulgaria: Tempest in a Teapot," in Reforms in the Soviet and Eastern European Economies, ed. L. A. D. Dellin and Hermann Gross (Lexington: Lexington Books, 1972), pp. 39-58.

2. Carl H. McMillan, Changing Perspective In East-West Commerce (Lexington: Heath, 1974), p. 27.

3. Bogoslav Dobrin, Bulgarian Economic Development Since World War II (New York: Praeger, 1973), p. 131.

4. Ibid., pp. 27-28.

5. Radoslav Selucky, Economic Reforms in Eastern Europe: Political Background and Economic Significance (New York: Praeger, 1972), pp. 156-57.

6. Unless otherwise noted, the information in this section is gleaned from Ota Sik, "Czechoslovakia: Prohibitive Odds," in Reforms in the Soviet and Eastern European Economies, ed. L. A. D. Dellin and Hermann Gross (Lexington: Lexington Books, 1972), pp. 59-78.

7. Edward Taborsky, "Czechoslovakia's Economic Reform: Balance Sheet of the First Year," East Europe 17 (April 1968): 20.

8. Otto Ulc, "Czechoslovakia: The Great Leap Backward," in The Politics of Modernization in Eastern Europe, ed. Charles Gati (New York: Praeger, 1974), p. 105.

9. Selucky, op. cit., p. 92.

10. Henry Wilcox Schaefer, Comecon and the Politics of Integration (New York: Praeger, 1972), p. 69.

11. "Czechoslovakia Eyes Western Sources For Up-to-Date Technology, Equipment," Commerce Today 4 (April 15, 1974): 31.

12. Unless otherwise noted, the information in this section is gleaned from Selucky, op. cit., pp. 57-78.

13. McMillan, op. cit., p. 26.

14. Karl C. Thalheim, "The Development of the East German Economy in the Framework of the Soviet Bloc," in Eastern Europe in Transition, ed. Kurt London (Baltimore: Johns Hopkins, 1966), p. 164.

15. Unless otherwise noted, the information in this section is gleaned from William F. Robinson, The Pattern of Reform in Hungary: A Political, Economic and Cultural Analysis (New York: Praeger, 1973), pp. 4-5, 100-95.

16. Selucky, op. cit., pp. 139-40.

17. Ibid., pp. 140-42.

18. United States Department of Commerce, "Trading In Hungary," Overseas Business Reports OBR 74-32 (July 1974): 2.

19. Willy Linder, "Hungary: Marching Forward," in Reforms in the Soviet and Eastern European Economies, ed. L. A. D. Dellin and Hermann Gross, (Lexington: Lexington Books, 1972), p. 82.

20. Joseph Szabados, "Hungary's NEM: Promises and Pitfalls," East Europe 17 (April 1968): 31.

21. Michael Gamarnikow, "Poland: On Again -- Off Again," in Reforms in the Soviet and Eastern European Economies, ed. L. A. D. Dellin and Hermann Gross (Lexington: Lexington Books, 1972), p. 93.

22. Ibid., pp. 94-95.

23. Ibid., pp. 95-96.

24. Ibid., pp. 102, 105, 107-09.

25. Janusz G. Zielinski, Economic Reforms in Polish Industry (London: Oxford University, 1973), pp. 310-12.

26. U. S. Department of Commerce, "Poland," Foreign Economic Trends ET 74-017 (April 1974): 5.

27. Claus D. Rohleder, "Rumania: The Laggard," in Reforms in the Soviet and Eastern European Economies, ed. L. A. D. Dellin and Hermann Gross (Lexington: Lexington Books, 1972), p. 120.

28. Selucky, op. cit., p. 152.

29. R. V. Burks, "The Rumanian National Deviation: An Accounting," in Eastern Europe in Transition, ed. Kurt London (Baltimore: Johns Hopkins, 1966), p. 97.

30. Trond Gilberg, Modernization in Romania Since World War II (New York: Praeger, 1975), p. 160.

31. Iancu Spigler, Economic Reform In Rumanian Industry (London: Oxford University, 1973), pp. 18-19, 58.

32. Zygmunt Nagorski, Jr., The Psychology of East-West Trade (New York: Mason and Lipscomb, 1974), p. 115.

33. Willy Sellekaerts, "Economic Reforms in Eastern Europe," MSU Business Topics 18 (Autumn 1970): 20-21.

34. Roger E. Kanet, "Modernizing Interaction Within Eastern Europe," in The Politics of Modernization in Eastern Europe: Testing the Soviet Model, ed. Charles Gati (New York: Praeger, 1974), p. 285.

35. Sandor Ausch, Theory and Practice of CMEA Cooperation, (Budapest: Academiai Kiado, 1972), pp. 69-70.

36. Sellekaerts, op. cit., p. 21.

37. Cyril E. Black, "Eastern Europe in the Context of Comparative Modernization," in The Politics of Modernization in Eastern Europe: Testing the Soviet Model, ed. Charles Gati (New York: Praeger, 1974), p. 33.

38. Thalheim, op. cit., pp. 157-58.

39. Adolf Hermann, "Can Comecon Integrate?," East Europe 18 (May 1969): 15.

40. Janos Fekete, "The Role of Monetary and Credit Policy in the Reform of Hungary's Economic Mechanism," in Money and Plan: Financial Aspects of East European Economic Reforms, ed. Gregory Grossman (Los Angeles: University of California, 1968), p. 67.

41. William R. Kintner and Wolfgang Klaiber, Eastern Europe and European Security (New York: Dunellen, 1971), p. 50.

42. Sellekaerts, op. cit., p. 22.

43. Selucky, op. cit., pp. 43, 55.

44. J. Wilczynski, The Economics of Socialism (London: Allen and Unwin, 1970), pp. 27-28.

45. Kanet, op. cit., p. 186.

46. Wolfgang Klaiber, "East-West Trade and U.S. Objectives in Eastern Europe," in East-West Trade and the Technology Gap: A Political and Economic Appraisal, ed. Stanislaw Wasawski (New York: Praeger, 1970), p. 209.

47. Spigler, op. cit., p. 19.

48. Viktor Meier, "Schwierige Integration im Ostblock," Frankfurter Allgemeine Zeitung, July 16, 1975, p. 9.

49. Sellekaerts, op. cit., p. 22.

50. Ausch, op. cit., p. 14.

51. Hermann, op. cit., p. 18.

52. Michael Gamarnikow, "Introduction: Economics and Politics," in Reforms in the Soviet and Eastern European Economies, ed. L. A. D. Dellin and Hermann Gross (Lexington: Lexington Books, 1972), p. 14.

53. Robinson, op. cit., p. 181.

PART II

INCONVERTIBILITY AND BILATERALISM

INTRODUCTION

Wolfgang Schmitz contends that

> "The great achievements of the world economy, which have been documented in the rapid rise and expansion of prosperity, are convertibility of currencies and free international exchange of goods and services. Convertibility and multilateralism allow for the application of the principle of efficiency in the international economic and monetary field, and they—and they alone—lead to an optimum combination of production factors without being restricted by national frontiers. These factors make it possible for small countries, too, to participate in the international division of labour and, consequently, in growing world prosperity."[1]

In recognition of the past and present unsatisfactory state of affairs, which finds the Comecon nations persistently trying to overcome the ill effects of inconvertibility and bilateralism, the CMEA monetary problem was at the top of the agenda of the 24th meeting of the council in May 1970.[2] Still, achievement of any type of extensive convertibility and multilateralism among bloc members seems to be a very distant aim. The creation of the CMEA International Bank for Economic Cooperation, although a positive step, was clearly not a sufficient measure to permit free movement of capital or unimpeded flow of commercial transactions, not even among the socialist nations. There is as yet no uniform price system, the bulk of trade is still bilateral in nature, and the ruble is far from being an international currency. Furthermore, the multilateral clearing system within the CMEA is basically restricted to the trade of consumer goods, while capital goods, tools, machines, and factory equipment, which are in shorter supply, are traded almost exclusively in bilateral trade agreements.[3]

We should not really be too surprised in our wondering about why the CMEA has so far failed in its efforts to progress toward a more satisfactory system. For one thing, it took the more advanced capitalist systems some 15 years after the war to achieve convertibility, and that with considerable external help. Also, there is quite a difference in level of development that marked the capitalist countries and the socialist countries immediately following the war. Furthermore, the bilateral system of Comecon is such that it would be impossible to switch over to full convertibility even if adequate gold and foreign exchanges reserves were available. For the CMEA to go from a bilateral to a multilateral system would require fundamental qualitative changes in the domestic economies of the individual countries, as well as in their external relations. Specifically, they would have to do away with two properties of the entire directive plan instructions system—the isolation of the domestic price level from international prices, and the system of directive export and import instructions.[4]

Thus, whatever the positive effects of initial steps towards industrialization taken by the members of Comecon, the long-term effects have had a definitely restrictive nature. Several things can be learned from the historical development of convertibility and multilateralism in the capitalist world. First, it is necessary to largely abolish the administrative import restrictions which were found necessary during and immediately following the war. Second, the least developed countries must receive assistance from those in a more tenable position. Third, relative freedom of intraregional trade is necessary. Credits to bridge trade deficits and an adequate amount of working capital are necessitated. Such would prove suitable for temporary balance of payments problems, but to prevent permanent, or structural, indebtedness, a connection must be created between the system of settlements and a convertible currency. Underlying all these conditions is the necessity of establishing a sound internal economic system to assure a relative equilibrium. When these conditions are met, regional multilateralism will promote the introduction of general convertibility. In addition, general convertibility requires, above all, an equilibrium of international payments, realistic rates of exchange, and the existence of substantial currency reserves.[5]

To be sure, there are definite advantages to bilateralism. Such a balancing of trade facilitates economic planning and reduces the need for currency transactions to the minimum, which, in light of the shortage of foreign reserves among the CMEA countries, is a valid consideration. In addition, bilateralism is a potent instrument of foreign policy. However, the immediate cause of Comecon bilateralism at the outset was its sheer inevitability. The disadvantages of bilateralism are apparent. It erodes the gains from international trade, since its capacity is dependent on the weaker partner. Of less importance are the administrative costs of negotiation and settlement, the insulation of economies, the protection of domestic industries, and so on. Basically, it is fact that multilateralism provides much more potential for economic growth.[6]

There are many factors which foster the continuation of bilateralism. Inconvertibility is probably the greatest factor. A second factor is the tendency among bloc countries to strive for overall balance of payments, which they mistakenly equivocate with bilateral balance. We have already seen the subordinate role which exports play to imports, and under such conditions, there is no strong incentive to create overall export surplus. A third factor encouraging bilateralism is the position of the economically stronger countries, since it improves their terms of trade.[7] Additionally, the international mechanism of the CMEA integration hinders multilateralization in many ways. Interest rates are so low that they encourage deficit rather than surpluses in the balance of payments, particularly since a system of clearing has not been satisfactorily worked out. No country accepts payment from another country voluntarily in the form of a balance with a third member, since they cannot use it to buy commodities needed to meet their real demands. Under such a system, convertibility cannot be established because convertibility would imply that all types of commodities could be purchased.[8] As much as this negates attempts towards multilateralism, it also is having the effect of stifling even bilateral trade among the Comecon members. That is, if one year's surplus is found to be rather worthless towards the acquisition of needed imports, the tendency in the following year would be to limit exports.[9]

For years, Western sources have ignored the implications of Eastern European inconvertibility and bilateralism, perhaps due in part to other overriding issues such as those of political, strategic, and even ethical questions concerning trade with the East. Also, East-West trade had been almost devoid of exchange risks due to the extensive use of Western currencies for such trade, and due to the excellent reputation of CMEA for prompt payment and strict adherence to contract stipulations.[10] Only recently are we discovering that the entire economic structure and system of the CMEA economies are quite incompatible with Western notions of trade. Accordingly, it would be advantageous to consider more closely some of the factors relevant towards the realization of both convertibility and multilateralism among the CMEA members. As we shall see, and in spite of Comecon assertions to the contrary, there seem to be insurmountable blocks along the way, at least in the foreseeable future.

NOTES

1. Wolfgang Schmitz, "Convertibility, Multilateralism and Freedom: A Concept for Recovery and Prosperity," in <u>Convertibility</u>,

Multilateralism and Freedom, ed. Wolfgang Schmitz (New York: Springer, 1972), p. ix.

2. Wolfgang Schmitz, "Monetary Dynamic Forces in East and West: Important Developments in the Seventies," in Convertibility, Multilateralism and Freedom, ed. Wolfgang Schmitz (New York: Springer, 1972), p. 228.

3. Kazimierz Grzbowski, "Organization and Conduct of Foreign Trade in Countries With State-Planned Economies: Comecon," in East-West Business Transactions, ed. Robert Starr (New York: Praeger, 1974), p. 130.

4. Sandor Ausch, "Problems of Bilateralism and Multilateralism in the External Trade and Payments System of the CMEA Countries," in Foreign Trade in a Planned Economy, ed. Imre Vajda and Mihaly Simai (Cambridge: Cambridge University, 1971), pp. 61, 78.

5. Sandor Ausch, Theory and Practice of CMEA Cooperation (Budapest: Academiai Kiado, 1972), pp. 152-53.

6. J. Wilczynski, Socialist Economic Development and Reforms (New York: Praeger, 1972), pp. 273-75.

7. Franklyn D. Holzman, Foreign Trade Under Central Planning (Cambridge: Harvard University, 1974), pp. 148-50.

8. T. Kiss, "The Development of the Forms of Economic Relations in the CMEA Integration," in The Market of Socialist Economic Integration, ed. T. Kiss (Budapest: Akademiai Kiado, 1973), p. 121.

9. J. Soldaczuk, "Trade and Cooperation Among CMEA Member Countries," in The Market of Socialist Economic Integration, ed. T. Kiss (Budapest: Akademiai Kiado, 1973), p. 140.

10. Gunter Dufey, "Financing East-West Business," Columbia Journal of World Business 9 (Spring 1974): 37.

CHAPTER

4

FACTORS RELEVANT TOWARD THE REALIZATION OF CONVERTIBILITY

PRICES

The basic obstacle to both convertibility and multilateralization is the absence of a rational price system. That is, only prices which reflect cost-preference conditions can provide a solid basis for the maximization of gains from international trade based on comparative advantage. As we have noted, each of the reforms which have taken place has had to deal with this very factor. At any rate, to the extent that the enterprises have been truly given more authority in the decentralization schemes, they are in a better position to react to changing price and demand functions.

Nevertheless, even considering only the internal relations of socialist economies, it is clear that the functions of production and sales are generally separated from each other. As far as external relations are concerned, the links between domestic and foreign-trade prices have been severed. For the large part, foreign trade organizations have had their performance measured at official domestic prices rather than the actual prices of foreign markets. Since export and import transactions have been centrally planned and dictated, the individual enterprises have not been able to consider existing comparative advantages. Until recently, about 60 to 70 percent of intra-CMEA trade was transacted under bilateral agreements covering a span of five years, in which the prices were fixed. (This policy was not changed until January 1975, when the CMEA decided to establish prices annually instead of every five years; the prices still lag somewhat, however, since they are based on the average world prices for the previous five years).[1] Finally, the system of stable foreign-trade prices is not only convenient, but totally necessary considering the institutional elimination of market mechanisms that could regulate such prices. Were the prices not fixed and stable, it could seriously disrupt the national plans of the partners, for imbalances could not be easily offset by suddenly changing national plans in midstream to provide the sought after balance.[2]

This break between domestic and external prices among the CMEA member nations has the consequence that their markets are imperfect in the economic sense, and as a rule do not take part in the shaping of regional prices. That is, since the prices do not reflect real cost-benefit circumstances, it is recognized that they are less than optimal. The same, of course, is true with internal prices. Domestic prices are geared to encourage the consumption of some goods and to discourage that of others, in order to implement the national plan. The system of planned prices is created with little regard for costs of production, prices in other bloc countries, or world prices. When goods are imported or exported, the prices are listed in the accounting system as domestic prices, and the foreign trade sector achieves gains or losses accordingly. The deficit is in essence a subsidy to the domestic producer, and the overall result is that it is extremely difficult to evaluate the effectiveness of the foreign trade sector.[3]

Socialist economists, as a whole, have agreed that price reform is a must. Generally, they agree also on the following. Prices must be determined in free competitive markets or derived from the optimal plan. The combination of all resources to production must be accepted as cost and reflected in the prices. There should be a closer correspondence between retail and producers' prices. Prices must be fairly flexible to respond to supply and demand conditions. Domestic prices of internationally traded products must be linked to those prevailing in world markets.[4]

The price reforms in the several countries have, in fact, shown tendencies in these directions. For one thing, the Marxian concept of "production price" as distinct from "value" has been adopted. Second, there has been the tendency to raise producers' prices to eliminate the need for planned deficits. Third, marginal concepts have been introduced. Fourth, prices which are centrally fixed are more subject to periodic revision in light of changing costs and demand. Fifth, the degree of insulation between retail and producers' prices has been reduced. Finally, there has been a considerable decentralization in some sectors in the determination of prices.[5]

Nevertheless, there are at least five major shortcomings in the context of profit as a criterion of enterprise efficiency in Comecon. There are substantial divergencies of the prices from social cost, and this varies in each of the countries. Since socialist central planning is incompatible with consumer's sovereignty, the consumer's preferences are not fully taken into consideration. Different planned prices are administered for different types of buyers and sellers for identical products. The complex price systems distort the prices, which, in the more dynamic economies, has multiplying effects. Although the state-initiated price changes have limitations, it is very often that other than economic considerations gain the upper hand.[6]

Even the socialist economists are well aware of the impossibility of the state's establishing accurate prices. In Czechoslovakia, for instance, there are about 1.5 million concrete prices that, in all right, ought to be changed all the time. When one considers the chore of correlating these prices as they all move, the complicatedness of the procedure becomes apparent. Of perhaps even more significance is the fact that only the producers themselves are in a position to gain the information quite necessary for the establishment of prices on any given product.[7]

The process is further complicated by the existence of four sets of prices. Programming prices are used for the construction of internally consistent plans, and for aggregation only. Shadow or accounting prices are used in investment and foreign-trade effectiveness calculations only. Operational prices are used in the process of plan fulfillment, basically as an information carrier. Finally, consumer goods prices are used which are, in principle, market-clearing prices for consumer goods.[8] Such a system, in which the functions of the price system would be confined to aggregation and control, was much more successful when all producer and consumer goods were strictly rationed, as upon the founding of Comecon. However, for the purpose of guiding enterprise managers to correct production decisions, prices must express current relative scarcities, must be kept up to date to reflect their link with current costs, and must, above all, be sensitive to supply and demand considerations.[9]

In the 1950s, to thwart price discrimination, the CMEA agreed that members would charge all CMEA trading partners the same price for the same commodity, with slight variations due to transportation costs. Those prices, in turn, are based on "world prices," as previously mentioned, although such world prices are cleansed from the capitalist distortions due to cyclical deviations, monopolistic power, and so on. Such use of world prices has not at all been wholeheartedly accepted by the member nations, particularly since, according to Marx, any developed country is always in a position to exploit a less-developed country. There is some question, however, as to the cleansing effects, since the resultant price is often far less rational than the original world price. Obviously, the CMEA countries cannot create a rational price system of their own until they individually have rational domestic prices.[10]

As it is, the domestic price formation in the individual countries must take into consideration the trends in the world market prices, while the foreign trade organizations of the countries in the CMEA must take into consideration at least three varying price levels: the domestic prices as well as the two foreign trade price levels (one in the socialist market and one in the capitalist market). Complications of all types arise in the forecasting as well as in the use of these prices.[11]

The use of world prices has many advantages and positive aspects, and some socialist economists contend that there is no better alternative. Indeed, it has been said, with tongue in cheek, that if the socialist states were to encompass the world, there could be no trade whatsoever, since there would be no mechanism for making an efficient choice between goods produced at home and abroad.[12] Those in favor of using world prices contend that the ratios of the prices to each other express the technological levels of the products in relation to the highest of standards; that through price changes, the development trends of the forces of production come to expression; that the direction of the movement of world market prices reflects changes in the international value relations; that the relative prices reflect the rational scale of production as well as the useful characteristics of the products, and so on. Additionally, it makes possible better reactions to price movements, and thus is a dynamic rather than static force.[13]

Nevertheless, there are sound reasons why such world prices should be at least modified. It is obvious that the application of world prices with no adjustment cannot always ensure cooperation based on reciprocal advantage. They are subordinated to business cycles, to speculative effects, monopoly interests, inflationary processes, and the price-wage spiral. For semifinished products and for many finished products, the world prices are not clearly ascertainable. Structural changes in the CMEA as well as long-range planning would often be handicapped by the use of world prices, and the optimal development of any given country's economy is not necessarily directly correlated to the movements in world prices. That is, the possibility of recognizing the special production conditions in any given nation must be fulfilled by a preference system.[14]

In addition, the use of world prices could definitely be detrimental to intrabloc trade. All of the bloc countries are in the position of being able to buy and sell in transactions with bloc countries and/or nonbloc countries. It is therefore obvious that it would be advantageous for a socialist country to sell in socialist markets only when the other socialist countries were buying in capitalist world markets, and vice versa; that assumes that bloc prices are not precisely equilibrated with world prices.[15]

Socialist prices, while they must remain flexible, must also be somewhat more stable than world prices, particularly during the phase of intergration through which Comecon is now going. Under the coordination of national economic plans and long-term multilateral and bilateral specialization agreements, the use of "free" price formation is impossible. Also, in regard to the stage of development, the production of many commodities in the CMEA countries is incapable of meeting increased demand, since increased production would require large-scale investment, and so on. In other words, the prices of the socialist international market must, of necessity, deviate somewhat from the "pure" world market prices, since the establishment and formation of the prices in Comecon must take numerous things into consideration which world prices would ignore.[16] If world prices are to be used as a guide, as they well could and should be, it must be clear that their use would be temporary rather than permanent, and limited rather than comprehensive. Efficient cooperation among the CMEA members must take into consideration the cost factors and production problems found in Comecon, not in the world at general.[17]

The members of Comecon are in quite some disagreement as to the eventual determination of prices. Labor-intensive economies, such as Bulgaria and Romania, prefer to use man-hours as a basis. The Czechoslovak and East German economists decidedly prefer the use of world prices, whereas the other, less-developed members seem agreeable to world prices only with numerous restrictions and alterations.[18] Even the method of price determination is disputed, should the basis of the decision be reached. That is, Poland and the Soviet Union prefer the retention of price fixing by central authority. The more advanced members prefer experimenting by the market mechanism, and the Romanians are being quiet about the whole thing, except for their persistent emphasis on sovereignty.[19]

In spite of all these considerations, it is probably Robert Campbell who most clearly reveals the fallacy of the CMEA using world market prices as the basis of their pricing system, in that he reminds us that the virtue of the price system in market economies is not that it provides perfect indexes of economic value, but that it performs an equilibrating function.[20] Although it would be erroneous to assume that capitalist prices could thus serve that function in a command economy, neither would it be correct to imply that the directives of socialist planning could be perfect on first elaboration or in all areas. In a free-market economy, equilibration mechanisms bring exports and imports into balance after certain changes. These mechanisms do not exist in a planned economy, and trade surpluses or deficits have little effect. The traditional macroeconomic foreign trade models which are valid in the West for economic performance analysis simply are not fully suitable for the CMEA countries.[21]

Until the mid-1960s, socialist prices were known for their rigidity, and this was considered an advantage. Since then, socialist planners have seen the advantages of flexible pricing. In fact, stability for its own sake in the face of changing conditions turned out to be a handicap. In a dynamic economy, prices must provide guidelines to the continuing process of substitution in accordance with changing cost-preference relationships. Consequently, the socialist systems devised four categories of prices based on the degree of permitted fluctuations. Fixed prices are held constant for longer periods, and are established generally for the products which have a substantial effect on the cost of living. Ceiling prices are allowed to fluctuate below a maximum level fixed by the state, and generally apply to raw materials and less essential items of household use where competition among sellers is possible and desirable. Free-range prices are those for which maximum and minimum limits are set for selected articles, so that the prices can move freely within that range. Finally, free prices are those allowed to fluctuate freely according to market supply and demand. In this category are found luxuries and many non-standardized things.[22]

There are many reasons why an entirely free price system cannot be introduced, even in regard to consumer goods. There are vast shortages on the supply side, and it will be years before the production potential catches up with demand, even assuming the development of a consumer-oriented economy. Also, there is the problem of the hidden excess of purchasing power, which, if released, would tend to produce a dangerous inflationary spiral. There have been years of acute shortages of high quality consumer goods, and that in addition to the impossibility of any significant private investment in property have created heavily swollen savings accounts in all of the more industrialized members of Comecon. These are not normal savings, but unrealized purchasing power. Released, that power would drive prices up considerably. Accordingly, great caution must be used in the gradual releasing of price restrictions in the Comecon countries.[23]

Basically, the solution to the pricing problems in Comecon finds three alternatives. Capitalist world market prices could be adopted without qualification, a distinct CMEA price structure could be created that is completely divorced from other world prices, or a combination of those two could be established. We have already referred to the benefits and disadvantages of using world prices as they are. The supporters of the CMEA-structured prices are generally the exporters of raw materials to the other members, and importers of manufactured products. The third decision, that of linking CMEA prices to the world prices but in such a manner that they reflect regional cost-preference conditions, seems by far the most tenable and feasible. Whatever the decision will turn out to be, it will vastly affect the countries under consideration, and we have repeatedly pointed out their high dependence of foreign trade, especially among themselves. Whatever the decision, most are in full agreement on the need for a uniformity of principles and procedures to govern the determination of prices, and, in turn, exchange rates.[24]

The important thing is not that the CMEA countries establish perfect price flexibility, but that they recognize the market process as the most efficient allocator of resources instead of central planning. Even though a certain amount of central planning remains, it is possible, through flexibility, to approach approximate market equilibrium prices, as well as to permit enterprises some freedom to react to market forces. Even in the West, maximization of profits is not the sole goal, and there is a constant trade-off between short-term and long-term profits. In any case, current market demand is not a perfect guide for future demand patterns, and state planning could be of definite use in investment patterns.[25]

For years, the economists of the bloc have been working on the formation of a socialist world price formation, one which would more closely reflect the regional costs of production. That the problems have no immediate solution in sight is evidenced by the fact that the task of such price formation was originally scheduled for completion in 1965, and is still far from complete.[26] In all likelihood, the eventual decision will, in fact, be a combination of market recognition and central planning.

Such a planned market economy will have prices which are essentially subject to the forces of supply and demand. There will, however, be limits of such prices, which will be determined by the domestic prices of the exporting and importing countries. For a considerably long time, the connection between prices of the CMEA and the outside world will be based on a dual "price coefficient," due to the difference in price levels and the domestic costs of production.[27] Basically, planned economy relying on market regulation means that in the microeconomic sphere the conditions that ensure the regulation of economic processes in accordance with the plan of the national economy can be established by market forces, which are in turn given direction by means of financial, price and income policy. That is, enterprise decisions would be made according to market forces, but those market forces would be controlled to a certain degree by state planning policy.[28]

Socialist economists are in disagreement as to the effects of past economic reforms on the resolution of the CMEA pricing problems. Some contend that the question of prices and the more important issues regarding the accounting mechanism, must be solved by the central bodies since these decisions affect the entire national economy. This faction recognizes that in the different socialist states, the enterprises have varying rights and spheres of authority; these economists consider such differences to be a serious handicap and impediment to the solution of price problems on the CMEA level.[29] Others strongly contend that the economic integration of the CMEA countries is not hindered by possible deviations in the internal systems of economic management in the countries. In fact, they contend, quite to the contrary, that such deviations may accelerate the participation of all countries in the international division of labor. They base their contentions on the theory that favorable or unfavorable effects on other countries occur not because of the management system, but are due to the unjustified or exaggerated preferential treatment of domestic production.[30] In other words, their contention amounts to the quite plausible assumption that the CMEA organization can be no stronger unless the individual members of which it is comprised are strengthened. This second group is closely in agreement with our own contention that any meaningful integration of Comecon must, of necessity, be preceded by substantial reform of the domestic economies.

In any event, it is clear that price must play an active role in the planned development of international specialization. Both on the macroeconomic and microeconomic levels, it is a prime determinant of efficiency. If prices fail to reflect profit opportunities and sensible investment choices on a national level, they can hardly be of help as indicators of opportunity costs and sensible decisions for Eastern Europe as a whole. To be effective indicators on the supranational level, those prices must be internationally comparable, a condition which is extremely difficult in the CMEA, given its economic insulation from the rest of the world and, in fact, even among its members.[31]

EXCHANGE RATES

Exchange rates in the CMEA countries are meaningless in the sense that they do not serve the purpose that exchange rates serve elsewhere. Although gold standards have been established, they are highly arbitrary, and the currencies are generally inconvertible. The gold standard does not reflect the value of the currencies, and the exchange rates do not reflect the purchasing power of the currencies. In a barter economy relying on planned foreign trade mechanisms and foreign exchange restrictions, such reflections are unnecessary, because neither exchange rates nor production costs regulate trade. Generally, trade with the West is settled in capitalist currencies, trade among CMEA members by the clearing ruble, and domestic prices of imports and exports are determined administratively; in the latter case, deficits and surpluses are leveled by budgetary procedures.[32] In general, the exchange rates have been so established as to insulate the internal economy from the influences from without. At any rate, as long as internal prices are disorderly and world prices are used as the basis for trade, and as long as both the composition and volume of trade are centrally controlled, the exchange rate is reduced to nothing but an accounting device.[33]

Characteristic of the Comecon countries' policies, each of the members has established multiple exchange rates. Thus there are not only different rates for intrabloc trade and nonbloc trade, but there are also different tourist rates. Even the tourist rates may easily be multiple, as in the case of Romania, which has more advantageous rates for tourists who exchange over 50 dollars than for those who do not exchange as much.[34] The rates of 1971, including those of the black markets, are found in Table 4.1. As can be determined from the fluctuations, the official basic rates, or those at which the value of trade is officially recorded, are furthest from equilibrium rates. Because of overvaluation, and due to the need to establish exchange rates which would promote exports and restrain imports, a substantial devaluation of the various currencies will be necessary once internal pricing adjustments can be made. Actually, it is the tourist rates now which are probably closest to actual purchasing power. At any rate, two steps must be taken towards the establishment of valid exchange rates if convertibility and multilateralism are desired: first, there needs to be further perfection of financial instruments and market relations to establish solid foundations for realistic parity rates; after that is accomplished, the parity rates must be further adjusted to ensure a balance of payments equilibrium.[35]

As the situation stands now, and as it has stood since the creation of the CMEA, the national exchange rates cannot be used as a fundamental and direct instrument for comparing the profitability of foreign trade transactions. As a result, this acts as a detriment to the further development of integration and specialization among the Comecon countries.[36] Complications of all sorts appear though when an attempt is made to establish suitable rates, for most socialist economists feel that a fixed rate of exchange would be incompatible for the CMEA bloc, and that instead, a type of exchange rate capable

TABLE 4.1

Exchange Rates of Socialist Currencies
(Units of national currency to U.S. $1.00)

Type of Exchange Rate	Bulgaria	Czechoslovakia	East Germany	Hungary	Poland	Romania
Official base rate	1.17	7.20	2.22	11.74	4.00	6.00
Implicit noncommercial rate for the ruble area	0.70	8.70	2.88	11.81	13.75	7.00
Noncommercial rates for hard-currency areas						
a) ordinary rate	2.00	14.36	4.20	30.00	24.00	18.00
b) bonus rate	—	16.20	—	—	40.00	—
Rate on non-commercial remittances from hard-currency areas	—	55.00	6.50	30.00	72.00	—
Other legal rates (clearing)	—	36.00	—	60.00	—	—
Black-market rate	3.70	60.00	15.00	55.00	120.00	35.00

Source: J. Wilczynski, Socialist Economic Development and Reforms, (New York: Praeger, 1972), p. 278.

of harmonizing with the deviations in the relative price levels of the different countries would be necessary.[37] This is complicated primarily by two overriding concerns: the irrational pricing systems in the countries, as well as the fact that their economies are in a transitional period. As it is now, joint Comecon projects, when translated into accounting entries, must be expressed in national currencies through the use of "coefficients," which vary depending on the countries involved, the industry concerned, and the materials used.[38] Thus, East Germany has different coefficients for each of seven monetary areas; in Czechoslovakia, a very complicated system of surcharges and discounts on two basic parities, graded as to categories of goods, is employed, with a fluctuation range of the dollar parity from minus 35 percent to plus 100 percent. In Hungary, the ruble is worth less than the dollar, whereas the opposite is true for the other Comecon nations, an interesting consequence of the use of such coefficients.[39]

The essence of valid exchange rates lies in the construction of economic links between domestic industries and the world market. Price relations are so divergent in the CMEA, however, that to apply a single "realistic" exchange rate to all partners and to all industries would throw the pattern of trade and industry into complete disarray.[40] Still, some progress is being made, if official attitudes can be considered as such. In mid-1974, for the first time, East Germans could legally possess Western currencies.[41] Of even more significance was Hungary's decision in mid-1971 to place Austro-Hungarian trade completely on a convertible currency basis; the Hungarians, however, are proceeding with extreme caution in regard to that agreement. In 1970 they had made a similar agreement with Yugoslavia, but the agreement did not materialize due to "unforeseen difficulties."[42] Unfortunately, we have been unable to locate information concerning the outcome of the agreement with Austria. In general, Czechoslovakia is more typical of CMEA countries in regard to exchange policies. Whereas import of foreign currency is unrestricted, both the import and export of Czechoslovak currency is forbidden, as is the dealing abroad with Czechoslovak money.[43] Meanwhile, exchange rate policy reform waits for reform on more basic issues.

INTERNATIONAL RESERVES

We have noted the balance-of-payments problems that the Comecon countries have in their trade with the industrial West. Closely associated with these problems are their levels of international reserves. However, it is possible to show on the surface an improvement in the overall balance-of-payments position, but at the same time to have a deterioration in the actual balance-of-payments position, due to the fact that import balances were in convertible currencies, while export balances were in inconvertible currencies, as in the case of Hungary.[44]

It is extremely difficult to determine CMEA reserve positions, since the Comecon members do not publish such figures. Western estimates of the reserves of the six countries under consideration, in aggregate, place the level at approximately $800 million, which is only sufficient to pay for no more than 5 to 10 percent of their annual imports. The proportion in the case of Western countries is usually 25 to 40 percent.[45] The lack of hard-currency reserves among the Comecon countries is one of the main concerns of Western trading partners, since the level of those reserves are now considered to be a minimum consistent with maneuverability in foreign trade.[46] As a result of their similar export structures and search for hard-currency reserves, the Eastern countries are inevitably in competition among themselves for Western markets.[47]

It is clear that the lack of reserves is not the major obstacle to the establishment of either convertibility or multilateralism, but it is essential in both cases to have such reserves. Not only is the low level of reserves a hindrance to the expansion of East-West trade, but it is also a factor which weighs more and more heavily on intrabloc trade. In principle, adequate planning would be assumed to reduce the need for reserves in the bilateral bartering type of trade characteristic of intrabloc commerce. On the other hand, the probability of substantial deviations is recognized by everyone, creating the need for such reserves, particularly of the ruble, if it is to become the common currency of the CMEA, a step beyond its present limited function as a mere accounting unit.[48]

In recognition of the problem, two CMEA institutions have been created. The International Bank for Economic Cooperation (IBEC) originally set its fixed capital at 300 million 1961 rubles ($333 million), which was contributed on the basis of volume of exports of its members. The contribution quotas in millions of transferable rubles were USSR, 116; East Germany, 55; Czechoslovakia, 45; Poland, 27; Hungary, 21; Bulgaria, 17; Romania, 16; and Mongolia, 3. Surpluses are dealt with in transferable rubles, against the wish of Poland, which argued unsuccessfully that all deposits should be made in gold or convertible currencies, and that all surpluses should be paid also in gold or convertible currencies. Similarly, the International Investment Bank is a creation of Comecon, whose initial capital of 1 billion rubles was to be proportioned as above, except that 70 percent was to be in transferable rubles and 30 percent in gold or convertible currencies.[49]

Many proposals have been made to overcome the problems of socialist reserves. One proposal is the creation of a new "socialist currency" linked by realistic exchange rates to domestic currencies and backed by the common monetary reserves and real resources of the CMEA. Another is that of a pool of international reserves consisting not of gold, but of hard currencies and hard commodities, which could be purchased with a trade surplus earned with any country. There are compromises of these two, suggesting combinations of gold, hard currency, and hard commodities. Others, perhaps more realistically, look to the West for help, as indicated by the charter of the IBEC, which permits all countries to contribute to the capital reserves of the bank. Bela Csikos-Nagy, one of the leading economists of the CMEA, contends that the CMEA countries should establish links with the monetary system in the West and gradually open their domestic markets to capitalist traders. Some Western economists recommend that a special fund be set up by Western interests for underwriting Eastern ventures.[50] Others contend that the USSR should simply carry out swap operations with Comecon countries in gold or free currencies against the transferable ruble, since the USSR is believed to have more than adequate gold supplies to do so.[51]

Some economists, without really considering the implications involved, simply contend that the CMEA countries should rebuild gold and exchange reserves by exporting more and importing relatively less, or borrow to substantial amounts from abroad. Actually, neither solution seems to be workable. The first involves reducing the rate of growth and the standard of living, complicated by the fact that the CMEA countries are in transitional stages of industrial development. The second solution depends on the willingness of many Western countries to accept such a proposal,[52] and we have already referred to the increasing hesitance of Western countries to do just that. Meanwhile, other considerations are slowing progress along these lines. A good example of this is offered in the case of Czechoslovakia. During 1974, Czechoslovakia suffered one of its largest hard-currency deficits in recent years (over $100 million). Basic needs for modern technology can be met only in the West, making it necessary for Czechoslovakia to continue substantial trading with the West. As far as intrabloc trade is concerned, a recent Soviet decision to raise prices on certain of its basic exports, effective January 1975, makes the Czechoslovak intrabloc position also less tenable, and hurts the country's chances for stable growth. This seriously affects Czechoslovakia's trade patterns with the West in several ways, but in relation to reserve levels, in a quite specific way: payment to the Soviets must be made partially in hard currency for purchases above stipulated quota limits.[53]

THE TRANSFERABLE RUBLE

Initially, local currencies were used for intrabloc trade not involving the Soviet Union. By 1955, the Soviet ruble was used throughout the CMEA for intrabloc accounts. Although at the time it was suggested widely that this was due to the instabliity of local currencies, it was thought later simply to be a step toward the total economic integration of the member countries. The ruble was not at first transferable when used as the bloc currency. Trade was conducted according to bilateral arrangements, and each pair of bloc countries was to exactly balance its trade with each other. Only insignificant imbalances occurred, and these were settled with either gold or convertible currencies. It was not until 1963 that the IBEC was established, and with it, a closed system of multilateral payments. To facilitate this, a new transferable ruble was created. For the first time, Poland (for example) could use a trade surplus with Bulgaria to settle a deficit with East Germany.[54]

The transferable ruble is not convertible; nor is it the national currency of the USSR. Basically, it is merely an accounting device used for clearing trade balances. The transferable ruble is created when payment for an export is recorded by the IBEC, and is eliminated when payment for an import is recorded. The value of the transferable ruble depends on the prices of imports and exports of the bloc countries, and varies accordingly. As these prices approach the goal of a single bloc price, which is highly unlikely in the foreseeable future, the value of the transferable ruble will approach the value of the internal ruble of the USSR. By late 1970, one Soviet author could refer to the transferable ruble as "the collective currency of the socialist countries," and it might well be that it eventually will become so.[55]

The multilateral accounting system which has been established is an inward-outward closed system. To the outside world, the system is closed completely, since there is no relation whatsoever between the clearing ruble and the monetary system of the capitalist world. It is also closed inward, for it is not integrated with the currencies of the members; it is detached from national foreign exchange relations and price relations. Subsequently, the intrabloc trade is still reduced to nothing much more than barter.[56]

Although the transferable ruble has a gold content equal to that of the Soviet ruble (0.829 ruble = U.S. $1), it is converted into the various national currencies through the use of an exchange multiplier, or a currency coefficient, which depends on the provisions applying in the countries concerned. It is, above all, not a medium of exchange.[57] Neither is the transferable ruble adequate in its function as a measure of value, due to the irrational pricing policies of the member countries. Like the clearing ruble before it, it expresses neither world prices nor domestic market prices.[58] In fact, the transferable ruble is not at all automatically transferable. It becomes transferable only if the transaction partners agree to such transferability. Subject to such agreements, each country needs to balance its accounts only with the group as a whole, instead of individually.[59] The gold value of the transferable ruble, then, remains a paper one, and the attempts to make it usable in trade with the West by granting at least partial recovery in gold have been to little avail.[60]

So far, the introduction of the transferable ruble has had no substantial effect on the trading patterns of the CMEA countries. It is mainly ineffective as a medium of international payments for three reasons: the countries still must balance their trading every year, foreign trade is still based on quotas, and there is no multinational settlement in free currencies. Its effectiveness awaits realistic exchange rates, which in turn await a rational system of internal prices.[61] The obstacles are so great that it is not even until 1980 that it is to be decided when unitary rates should be introduced, much less how.[62]

A transferable currency has been defined as one which is convertible only on a regional basis. Under such an assumption, it is perhaps more accurate to term the bloc currency as simply a clearing currency, since it does not even serve the function of accumulating wealth.[63] The ruble is convertible in no sense of the word, and transferable only in a very limited sense. As a result, it has been postulated that the USSR is not moving toward convertibility in the Western sense, but is attempting instead to set up a competing monetary system; this suggestion was made, however, before the recent efforts toward detente.[64] Perhaps a more valid assessment is that, to assure eventual convertibility, the only really effective way to improve financial arrangements would be to bypass the cumbersome transferable ruble accounting system altogether, and to settle such domestic expenditures in domestic currencies.[65]

Reform proposals in the area of the transferable ruble have been made frequently by the Poles. In their opinion, the main object of transferability is to prevent creditors' balances from being deprived of their usability. Therefore, they contend, exporting countries should have access to their credit balances, and debtors should be made to pay part of the outstanding claims in convertible currencies. Increasing percentages would be used both as to size of debit balances and time outstanding. However, the Polish delegates have not been able to win over support from the remaining members of Comecon.[66] Still, any long-term solution must depend on the support of nonbloc members. Accordingly, in October 1972 the IBEC Council improved the terms of participation in the transferable ruble settlement system for countries outside the IBEC. As a result, banks of nonmember countries participating in such settlements may receive transferable rubles in payment for goods delivered, as well as in payment for expenses involved in noncommercial transactions.[67]

PAYMENTS

Generally, payments of the CMEA members are organized in three separate ways, according to whether the payments are among themselves, as the bulk of them are, with the West, or with nonmember countries whose currencies are inconvertible. As mentioned, all trade agreements within Comecon use the transferable ruble as the unit of account. All payments are uniformly channeled through the IBEC, with the state bank usually in charge of the annual payments plan and the Foreign Trade Bank in charge of the day-to-day operating contacts with the IBEC. A separate foreign exchange budget is prepared for countries with convertible currencies, since those budgets require extremely close supervision of exchange earnings and negotiation of needed credit. For those nonmember countries with inconvertible currencies, all payments are cleared through accounts kept by the respective central banks. Due to the chronic shortage of hard-currency reserves, the CMEA members are generally willing to pay free currency at delivery only for economically essential goods, and more often than not, medium- to long-term supplier credit terms are sought with payment offered partly in convertible currencies, partly in merchandise deliveries.[68] Later, we shall consider the different types of such arrangements.

Intrabloc trade is largely bilateral, but bilateral balancing has been much less common in the CMEA countries' trade with other countries. Some currency areas, especially the sterling area and the European Payments Union, have been treated by the bloc as convenient reservoirs for multilateral balancing settlements. Several of the bloc members have agreements with Austria under which they are permitted under certain circumstances to make payment in convertible currency at an average 5 percent discount. Interestingly, Austria has not been too sold on the idea, and views the agreements somewhat negatively. The reason for such an attitude is that, by abandoning their bilateral clearing agreements, the Austrians lose control over their trade as such, since the Eastern partner is then free to buy elsewhere the goods which he would ordinarily buy from Austria. At any rate, the CMEA trade with the West is becoming more and more multilateral in nature.[69] Such convertible currency agreements, however, have not been widely introduced in the bloc's dealings with developing countries.[70]

In their dealings with the Western industrialized nations, the Eastern bloc countries are not much different from small developing countries, which operate mainly with major currencies and whose own currencies play a very small role in international trade. Theoretically, convertible currencies might be used for intrabloc trade. It does not work out that way in practice, however, for several reasons, two of which are the small level of reserves and the increased value of the convertible currencies outside the bloc.[71] In general, the possibility of multilateral transactions outside the bloc will in time have positive effects on progress towards multilateralism within the bloc.

COMMODITY INCONVERTIBILITY

Franklyn D. Holzman[72] sees the major feature of socialist problems not as that of currency inconvertibility, but of commodity inconvertibility. Currency inconvertibility, typical of capitalist-type diseases, can be temporarily cured by devaluation. Commodity inconvertibility, on the other hand, requires far-reaching economic reforms such as those to which we have referred: the opening up of domestic markets to foreign buyers and sellers, decentralization of planning, the establishment of rational internal prices, and so on. Commodity inconvertibility is seen as a substantial limitation on purchases by nonresidents, and is quite characteristic of the CMEA members. As to the chances of curing such inconvertibility in the near future, prospects are far from good, for to do so would mean a significant weakening of the CMEA as a supranational organization, and indications are that the trend is toward, instead of away from, integration, even if on a more or less superficial level. Nevertheless, it is apparent that the major causes of inconvertibility are becoming less severe. That is, structural imbalances are slowly but surely being corrected, the potential dangers of overfull employment are being recognized, shortages are less of a problem now than in the past, and all of these developments will eventually lead to the strengthening of the economies to the extent that they might indeed open up their area to more international trade.

NOTES

1. Viktor Meier, "Schwierige Integration im Ostblock," Frankfurter Allgemeine Zeitung, July 16, 1975, p. 9.
2. Sandor Ausch, Theory and Practice of CMEA Cooperation (Budapest: Academiai Kiado, 1972), p. 77.
3. Laszlo Zsoldos, Economic Integration of Hungary into the Soviet Bloc: Foreign Trade Experience (Columbus: Ohio State University, 1963), pp. 15-16.
4. J. Wilczynski, Socialist Economic Development and Reforms (New York: Praeger, 1972), p. 78.

5. Ibid., pp. 79-81.

6. J. Wilczynski, Profit, Risk and Incentives Under Socialist Economic Planning (London: Macmillan, 1973), pp. 105-08.

7. Ota Sik, "Czechoslovakia: Prohibitive Odds," in Reforms in the Soviet and Eastern European Economies, ed. L. A. D. Dellin and Hermann Gross (Lexington: Heath, 1972), p. 67.

8. J. G. Zielinski, On the Theory of Socialist Planning (London: Oxford University, 1968), p. 13.

9. John Michael Montias, Central Planning in Poland (Westport: Greenwood, 1962), pp. 190-91.

10. Nicolas Spulber, Socialist Management and Planning: Topics in Comparative Socialist Economics (Bloomington: Indiana University, 1971), pp. 11-12.

11. B. M. Shastitko and Y. S. Shiryaev, "Interrelations With Non-socialist Markets," in The Market of Socialist Economic Integration, ed. T. Kiss (Budapest: Akademiai Kiado, 1973), p. 164.

12. Jozef M. P. van Brabant, Essays on Planning in Eastern Europe (Rotterdam: Rotterdam University, 1974), p. 131.

13. Bela Csikos-Nagy, "Mutual Advantages In the Economic Cooperation," in The Market of Socialist Economic Integration, ed. T. Kiss (Budapest: Akademiai Kiado, 1973), pp. 182-83.

14. Ibid., p. 184.

15. Zsoldos, op. cit., p. 20.

16. A. Lyutov, "Economic Integration and the Socialist International Market," in The Market of Socialist Economic Integration, ed. T. Kiss (Budapest: Akademiai Kiado, 1973), pp. 53-54.

17. Y. Kormnov, "International Industrial Specialization," in The Market of Socialist Economic Integration, ed. T. Kiss (Budapest: Akademiai Kiado, 1973), p. 147.

18. Spulber, op. cit., p. 111.

19. Michael Gamarnikow, Economic Reforms in Eastern Europe (Detroit: Wayne State University, 1968), p. 80.

20. Robert Campbell, "On the Theory of Economic Administration," in Industrialization In Two Systems, ed. Henry Rosovsky (New York: John Wiley and Sons, 1966), p. 193.

21. Bogoslav Dobrin, Bulgarian Economic Development Since World War II (New York: Praeger, 1973), p. 101.

22. Wilczynski, Socialist Economic Development, op. cit., p. 88.

23. Gamarnikow, op. cit., pp. 78-79.

24. Wilczynski, Socialist Economic Development, op. cit., pp. 93-95.

25. George Garvy, "East European Credit and Finance in Transition," in Money and Plan: Financial Aspects of East European Eco-

nomic Reforms, ed. Gregory Grossman (Los Angeles: University of California, 1968), pp. 161-62.

26. Eugene Babitchev, "The International Bank for Economic Cooperation," in Money and Plan: Financial Aspects of East European Economic Reforms, ed. Gregory Grossman (Los Angeles: University of California, 1968), p. 145.

27. Ausch, op. cit., p. 132.

28. Bela Csikos-Nagy, Socialist Economic Policy (New York: St. Martin's, 1973), pp. 109-10.

29. Lyutov, op. cit., p. 55.

30. J. Wilcsek, "Interrelations Between the National Economic Management Systems and the Socialist International Market Mechanism," in The Market of Socialist Economic Integration, ed. T. Kiss (Budapest: Akademiai Kiado, 1973), p. 107.

31. Nish Jamgotch, Soviet-East European Dialogue: International Relations of a New Type?," (Stanford: Stanford University, 1968), p. 76.

32. Csikos-Nagy, Socialist Economic Policy, op. cit., pp. 221-22.

33. Franklyn D. Holzman, Foreign Trade Under Central Planning (Cambridge: Harvard University, 1974), pp. 143-44.

34. J. Wilczynski, The Economics of Socialism (London: Allen and Unwin, 1970), p. 181.

35. Wilczynski, Socialist Economic Development, op. cit., pp. 276-78.

36. J. Wesolowski, "Monetary and Financial Relations," in The Market of Socialist Economic Integration, ed. T. Kiss (Budapest: Adkademiai Kiado, 1973), p. 206.

37. K. Kover, "Internal Monetary Systems and Foreign Exchange Systems," in The Market of Socialist Economic Integration, ed. T. Kiss (Budapest: Akademiai Kiado, 1973), p. 214.

38. Babitchev, op. cit., p. 133.

39. Wolfgang Schmitz, "Monetary Dynamic Forces in East and West: Important Developments in the Seventies," in Convertibility, Multilateralism and Freedom, ed. Wolfgang Schmitz (New York: Springer, 1972), p. 232.

40. Adolf Hermann, "Can Comecon Integrate?," East Europe 18 (May, 1969): 18.

41. Heinz Brestel, "Wenn drueben einer Westgeld hat," Frankfurter Allgemeine Zeitung, June 14, 1975, p. 11.

42. William F. Robinson, The Pattern of Reform in Hungary: A Political, Economic and Cultural Analysis (New York: Praeger, 1973), pp. 135-36.

43. Karl Herman, "The Czechoslovak Socialist Republic," in East-West Business Transactions, ed. Robert Starr (New York: Praeger, 1974), p. 174.

44. Zsoldos, op. cit., p. 22.

45. Wilczynski, Socialist Economic Development, op. cit., pp. 284-85.

46. George T. French, "Problems in Conducting East-West Trade: One Company's Experience," in Financing East-West Business Transactions, ed. American Management Association, Inc. (New York: American Management Association, 1968), p. 13.

47. Michael Gamarnikow, "Is Comecon Obsolete?," East Europe 17 (April, 1968): 13.

48. O. Bogomolov, "The International Market of the CMEA Countries," in The Market of Socialist Economic Integration, ed. T. Kiss (Budapest: Akademiai Kiado, 1973), p. 34.

49. Glen Alden Smith, Soviet Foreign Trade: Organization, Operations, and Policy, 1918-1971 (New York: Praeger, 1973), pp. 152-53.

50. Wilczynski, Socialist Economic Development, op. cit., pp. 285-86.

51. Schmitz, op. cit., p. 231.

52. Zdzislaw M. Rurarz, "Polish Experience and Practices In East-West Trade," in East-West Trade: An Analysis of Trade Between Western Nations and the Soviet Bloc, ed. American Management Association, Inc. (New York: American Management Association, 1964), p. 50.

53. U.S. Department of Commerce, "Czechoslovakia," Foreign Economic Trends FET 75-053 (June 1975): 6.

54. Smith, op. cit., pp. 159-60.

55. Ibid., p. 160.

56. Csikos-Nagy, Socialist Economic Policy, op. cit., p. 220.

57. Andor Laszlo, "Monetary Policy: A Help to Fostering International Cooperation," in Convertibility, Multilateralism and Freedom, ed. Wolfgang Schmitz (New York: Springer, 1972), p. 127.

58. Wesolowski, op. cit., p. 206.

59. Wilczynski, Socialist Economic Development, op. cit., p. 288.

60. James A. Ramsey, "The 'Euroruble' -- Competition or Convertibility?," Columbia Journal of World Business 3 (November-December 1968): 62.

61. Schmitz, op. cit., pp. 228, 233.

62. "Comecon Integration Program," East Europe 20 (August 1971): 34-35.

63. Ausch, op. cit., p. 159.

64. Ramsey, op. cit., p. 66.

65. Henry Wilcox Schaefer, Comecon and the Politics of Integration (New York: Praeger, 1972), p. 167.

66. Schmitz, op. cit., p. 230.

67. Kazimierz Grzbowski, "Organization and Conduct of Foreign Trade in Countries With State-Planned Economies: Comecon," in East-West Business Transactions, ed. Robert Starr (New York: Praeger, 1974), p. 131.

68. John P. Morgan, "The Financial Aspects of East-West Trade," Columbia Journal of World Business 8 (Winter 1973): 54.

69. Ramsey, op. cit., p. 62.

70. Lothar J. Schultz and Clifford A. Rathkopf, Jr., "The German Democratic Republic," in East-West Business Transactions, ed. Robert Starr (New York: Praeger, 1974), p. 195.

71. Franklyn D. Holzman, "Future East-West Economic Issues," in The Future of the International Economic Order: An Agenda for Research, ed. C. Fred Bergsten (Lexington: Heath, 1973), p. 271.

72. Holzman, Foreign Trade Under Central Planning, op. cit., pp. 144-45, 222-23.

CHAPTER

5

FACTORS RELEVANT TOWARD THE REALIZATION OF MULTILATERALISM

Bilateralism is so closely associated with currency inconvertibility that no sharp distinction can be made between the causes and effects of one as compared to the other. Presently, we are concerned with institutions and developments which are generally related to bilateralism, whereas in the preceding section we were concerned with factors which were more specifically related to inconvertibility. The question of financing by credit, which is directly related to both, will be considered separately.

CMEA FINANCIAL AND BANKING INSTITUTIONS

The socialist countries have traditionally had a very restricted view of the role of money, and for years the main function of the banking system was to administer the distribution of finance for purposes which were predetermined in detail by the individual state plans. Since the accent has now shifted from extensive to intensive growth, however, a more flexible use of finance has assumed a strategic role, and monetary and banking policy has assumed increased importance.[1] Nevertheless, capital movements between the members have been of little significance, and when they occur, it is usually more to the advantage of the countries providing capital than of those receiving it. This, plus general disinterest in joint investment banks, is explained by the fact that the richer countries, given their own capital needs, do not wish to contribute in large measure to the development of the poorer countries, and thus aid potential competitors.[2] In addition to the increased role of banking, the recent economic reforms have affected banking in at least two other ways: there is greater functional specialization in serving different branches of industry, whereas earlier the institutional division of banking had been between short- and long-term financing; and there is a greater financial centralization, due not only to the increased importance of banking, but also to the increased independence of the enterprises.[3]

Each member of CMEA has Foreign Trade Banks which are in charge of all payments related to foreign trade and international service transactions, and which participate in the multilateral clearing arrangements of the intrabloc banks.[4] However, we are primarily concerned now with those intrabloc institutions.

The International Bank for Economic Cooperation (IBEC)

IBEC, founded in 1964, clearly represents an effort on the part of CMEA to foster multilateralism. Indeed, its goals are: the gradual multilateralization of intra-CMEA trade and payment obligations; the elimination of the stifling system of bilateral trade and payments policies; to provide for short-term credits to accommodate bilateral imbalances; and to ease the exchange between East and West. Of these four major goals, it has accomplished one, the extending of short-term credits. It has not at all succeeded in the substitution of multilateralism for bilateralism, since its principles did not even touch upon the old barriers to the multilateralization of intrabloc trade and payments. As a result, the bank has turned into nothing much more than a bookkeeping function of the bilateral patterns.[5]

On the other hand, it has been successful in certain aspects. After interest rates were increased in 1968 to induce borrowers to repay their credits on maturity, the turnover of the bank's resources was speeded up. The bank has established business relations with about 130 capitalist banks, and carries out substantial operations in gold and convertible currencies; between 1965 and 1970 the amount of these operations increased from $3 million to $15 million.[6] In spite of this, however, the financing of economic cooperation within Comecon has been the weakest aspect of the general plan for integration and industrial development of the member countries.[7] Since the bank developed into one which merely monitored fulfillment of intrabloc contracts and tried to tap Western money markets for additional reserves, it could not well serve its purpose of fostering integration and multilateralism; also, it had no sound method for judging the effectiveness of investment proposals, due to the pricing and monetary problems we have already discussed.[8] When money does not function as money, banks are ineffective.

International Investment Bank (IIB)

The IIB began operations in 1971 with the goal of partially financing investment projects in the CMEA to stimulate specialization and the socialist international division of labor. Better structured than the IBEC, the IIB has certain advantages: a substantial subscribed capital (over a billion rubles), 30 percent of which is in gold and convertible currencies; majority instead of unanimous voting; commercial interest rates; and the power to float bonds on nonsocialist markets. Initial contributions, however, had to be only 35 percent of the total allotted to each country. The main activity of the bank is to extend medium-(up to five years) and long-term (up to fifteen years) loans, and those for projects which the bank deems "interesting." Projects are considered on an ad hoc basis, with primary emphasis on what the project adds to CMEA integration, that is, for the entire community.[9]

Since its main purpose is to foster integration through specialization and joint efforts, most Western critics have been skeptical as to its potential. That is, the bank will not be an autonomous investment organization, but will only grant loans to national planning bodies which submit desirable projects. In essence, this means that the bank can enlarge on already planned activities, but will not instigate any of its own. As far as coordination of national plans, the nationalistic tendencies of the bloc will prevent the bank from having any supranational powers. In addition, it too, like the IBEC before it, must contend with the irrationality of the pricing system in its efforts to measure the desirability of given projects. Also, the problems of individual efforts at national development in contrast to regional development have been neglected.[10]

When the idea of the bank first came close to realization, it was thought by some critics to be merely a means by which the USSR could gain credits to improve the condition of its extractive industries.[11] It was also widely recognized by CMEA members that the bank would not solve all the old problems which they have slowly come to recognize in their efforts towards multilateralization; even after full payment of contributions, the guaranteeing of a commodity cover for the transferable ruble, and eventual full convertibility, it is known that the sum of 1 billion rubles would not be nearly sufficient for even the most basic investment needs of the Comecon countries.[12] On the other hand, the bank is considered to have not only an economic, but also a very important psychological effect on the East European countries. It could, in fact, lead to a new way of thinking not only about Comecon integration in general, but about a new and desirable supranational concept of efficiency, coordinated with national concepts and respecting national differences.[13] Nevertheless, the successful operation of the bank will depend on the achievement of universal usability of its resources, which means full convertibility of the capital quotas of the member countries.[14] Until that occurs, psychological advantages will be of little avail.

Eastern Commercial Banks in the West

A significant recent development is the move by the two CMEA banks and by the banks of individual CMEA states to tap the Eurocurrency market. In 1972, the two CMEA banks borrowed $200 million in the Western Europe money market; since the smaller members of Comecon share in these ventures, they thus gain from having the credit of the USSR behind them, which probably makes the terms more advantageous and the credit easier to obtain.[15] Table 5.1 shows the borrowing and lending on the London Eurocurrency market by the members of the CMEA in 1972 and 1973. We shall discuss credit in a later chapter.

However, following the Soviet example, CMEA countries are also establishing some banks in the West, in some cases with Western ownership participation. Attracting hard-currency deposits, these banks participate in Western banking consortia and enter the Eurodollar and Eurobond markets, with their main task being to facilitate and finance East-West trade and to sponsor cooperative ventures. In 1973, Romania, Poland, and Hungary all had such banks in operation.[16] Not only do such banks give the national foreign trade banks considerably more financial latitude than before and a higher profile in international banking circles, but they also make possible both advice and expertise which the countries would otherwise not receive.[17]

WORLD FINANCIAL AND BANKING INSTITUTIONS

Unquestionably, membership in the International Monetary Fund (IMF) and the International Bank for Reconstruction and Development (IBRD) would stimulate multilateralism among the Comecon countries. Nevertheless, until recently the members of the CMEA have tended, for the large part, to shy away from those organizations, although it would be a big step forward toward the convertibility of national currencies. Such ties would lead to immediate

TABLE 5.1

Borrowing and Lending on the London Eurocurrency Market by European CMEA Countries, 1972 and 1973
(millions of current U.S. dollars)

	1972			1973			Increase, 1973 over 1972
	Borrowing	Lending	Balance	Borrowing	Lending	Balance	
USSR	533	485	- 48	1,370	811	- 559	- 511
Bulgaria	192	26	-166	276	5	- 271	- 105
Czechoslovakia	50	120	70	108	122	14	- 56
East Germany	194	86	-108	446	65	- 381	- 273
Hungary	334	86	-248	430	84	- 346	- 98
Poland	180	108	- 72	574	146	- 428	- 356
Romania	96	7	- 89	146	26	- 120	- 31
CMEA Total	1,579	918	-661	3,350	1,259	-2,091	-1,430

Source: Carl H. McMillan, ed., Changing Perspectives in East-West Commerce (Lexington, Mass.: Heath, 1974), p. 145.

problems. For one thing, membership involves an official obligation to provide certain detailed information on financial status, and the CMEA countries have been prone to regard their gold and hard-currency holdings as state secrets. Additionally, it is felt that the USSR is opposed to the entry by CMEA countries to these organizations.[18] Romania has led the way against such obstacles, becoming accepted for membership in December 1972 for both the IBRD and IMF. With the IBRD, Romania has been granted the status of a developing country, and can thus obtain low-interest World Bank Development loans and qualifies for assistance in the form of access to the IMF's Special Drawing Rights Account.[19]

Romania has already made good use of its memberships. It drew on $47.5 million in December 1972 to alleviate problems due to a bad crop year, and in July 1974, it obtained two loans from the World Bank, totaling $130 million. Romania's entry might well have laid the stage for consideration of other CMEA countries, since the hurdles of technical nature have been passed. Nevertheless, it is widely felt that the attitude of the USSR shall be the deciding factor as far as the other CMEA members are concerned, for they have not shown the independent spirit of the Romanians in standing up against both CMEA and Soviet Policy.[20]

INTERNATIONAL COMMERCIAL COOPERATION

The CMEA countries have shown much more interest in commercial cooperation than in monetary cooperation, and, like the IMF and IBRD, the General Agreement on Tariffs and Trade (GATT) has attempted to adapt its rules to encourage East European participation. Poland, Romania, and Hungary are the only three centrally planned economies which are active members of GATT. Czechoslovakia became a contracting party in 1947 before it was a centrally planned economy, but has not participated in the agreement since its socialization.[21] A reference to the cases of Poland and Hungary illustrates the concessions which must be made by both sides when a member of Comecon becomes a contracting party to GATT.

Poland had enjoyed only observer status since 1957, since it could not claim that its economy operated on a basis comparable to that of a market-oriented system; moreover, its absence of a tariff structure complicated things since GATT places considerable emphasis on tariff concessions among its members. Accordingly, Poland offered to introduce a tariff schedule, a fact which the organization's membership considered pointless, and a mere formality, since Polish prices were not determined by supply and demand, and Polish foreign transactions were still the result of administrative decisions. What eventually led the membership to accept Poland for full standing was Poland's readiness to adjust its economic development plans to ensure a specific rate of expansion in the internal market for goods from other GATT members. Among the most significant terms which conditioned Poland's final admission, as of October 18, 1967, was a commitment to increase by 7 percent annually over a period of three years the value of imports from other members.[22]

The case of Hungary was similar. The main issue was the bilateral nature of trade agreements, for GATT principles insist that all GATT members be accorded the same conditions for entry on the Hungarian market. Second, market research into Hungarian foreign requirements is difficult to undertake because of the complicated system of direct and indirect controls, meaning that trade of the West with Hungary would be mostly the result of Hungarian initiatives and efforts of large capitalist firms. Still, entry into GATT by Hungary, or by any centrally planned economy, is a great boost to efforts towards multilateralization. The conditions of entry should lead to a gradual elimination of the present system of direct interventions, and to the gradual simplification of the several indirect control instruments.[23]

TRADE AGREEMENTS AND PROTOCOLS

Two trends are noticeable in the CMEA trade agreements and protocols. First, such agreements have tended to become less and less specific; second, an increasing amount of trade is being undertaken outside the confines of such agreements, particularly with the industrialized nations of the West. Even in intrabloc trade, above-quota trade is not uncommon, and is often settled on a multilateral basis in convertible currencies.[24] Such trade tends to destroy the basic motivations for bilateralism, that is, the exchange of goods without foreign exchange payment, and forcing your partner to buy as much from you as you from him. As far as East-West trade is concerned, there had always been three types of arrangements which allowed for at least a degree of multilateralism: the transfer of balances to third countries by mutual consent; explicit provisions for re-exporting to third countries; and planned triangular trade. However, one of the main obstacles to the transferability of clearing balances has been the absence of a multilateral clearing system among the bloc countries themselves.[25]

Britain and Germany, the two Western countries having the largest amount of trade with the CMEA bloc, have very largely abandoned bilateralism with the bloc countries. The biggest impediment is still the lack of convertible currencies in the bloc.[26] Earlier, East European exports to the West were subject to a strict quota system; that system no longer occupies the place of importance which it once did, and an extensive free listing of commodities that can be sold in the West under open general licensing has been developed.[27] All of these are significant steps in the direction of multilateralization and normalization of trade relations.

CMEA MODIFICATIONS TO BILATERALISM

In general, the attempts of the CMEA to establish full-scale multilateralization have failed miserably. However, certain modifications to the trade patterns have been made which have proved advantageous. Re-exporting has been one modification, although its usage has been very limited, and it involved uneconomical transportation and administrative costs. Swing credits, a system of mutual borrowing and lending in financing yearly trade, has had obvious advantages, and is widely used, although CMEA agreements limit such swing credits to 3 percent of intra-CMEA exports of the previous trade periods. One way around that limit has been to convert the swing credits to long-term credits, a step that was widely used in Soviet-Czechoslovak economic relations in the early 1960s. Additionally, the irrational pricing systems of the member countries have made possible much maneuverability, since discriminatory accounting for bargaining purposes has been practiced; some actual price discrimination has occurred in order to clear bilateral trade.[28]

Resource reallocation has been used very ineffectively in the CMEA bloc. Both capital and labor movements have been at minimum levels, and this area of improvement can and should be much accelerated. The only really effective movement of resources has been that of technology, although as a whole, technological development in the Comecon area is much behind that of the West. Market separation has played an important role in the general trend toward multilateralism, although negatively. That is, the earlier stress on autarkic development has slowed down progress away from bilateralism. The increase in nonbloc trade partners, however, has been a concrete and psychological boost to multilateralism. Also, past frustration with the bilateral structure has led to multilateralization. The policy of industrialization in the member countries led to inevitable conflicts of interests in the negotiation of bilateral trade agreements. The exporters of primary goods have been particularly helped by such factors as tied sales, low-interest credit, changes in the distribution and structure of trade. Finally, both political and strategic motives have influenced production and trade beyond the economic arguments and requirement of strict bilateralism. Such political and strategic motives have set limits to intrabloc trade.[29]

MARKET FACTORS

Markets—both buyers' and sellers'—have a profound influence on the efforts of the CMEA members to increase multilateralism. For one thing, we have noticed that Western trading partners have been gradually relaxing their quotas on imports from the CMEA. Such obstacles to East-West trade are certainly worthy of note, but they are not of major concern as far as CMEA markets are concerned. Few tariffs, for example, are maintained by the bloc countries, but that has little to do with the conduct of their trade, since access to their markets had been effectively denied by other means. In theory, tariff reductions increase the extent to which comparative advantage is operative in world trade, but with the Eastern method of economic decision making, such is simply not the case.[30] Still, there can be no question that Western access to Eastern markets has increased considerably in recent years.

Since the introduction of the economic reforms, most bloc economists assume the operation of market mechanisms in at least three areas: the market for the distribution of consumer goods, the financial market, and the external market. There are three major grounds on which the introduction of market forces have been welcomed in the CMEA. First, socialist economics have been historically concentrated on macroeconomic issues, and they have failed to a great extent at the microeconomic level. The introduction of market mechanisms will help to overcome this problem. Second, the operation of the market mechanism is necessary for the continual verification and correction of planned decisions. Finally, the market provides a discipline in the form of competition, and will spur the efficiency which, as we have already noted, is quite essential now that the CMEA countries have changed from an extensive to an intensive growth pattern.[31]

Whatever the case, a genuine market within the CMEA is quite necessary for eventual multilateralism. Practices of the past must be avoided, such as the dependence of the CMEA members on the USSR both as a buyers' and sellers' market. An example of that was the establishment of steel industries fully dependent on Soviet ore that operate at such high cost they cannot sell on outside markets.[32] As to buyers' markets, shortages are becoming much less common in the CMEA as their economies are attaining greater capacities for production, both quantitatively and qualitatively, and as more experience is being gained in monetary and incomes policy.[33]

NOTES

1. J. Wilczynski, Socialist Economic Development and Reforms (New York: Praeger, 1972), pp. 144-45.
2. M. A. G. van Meerhaeghe, International Economic Institutions (New York: St. Martin's, 1971), pp. 223-24.
3. J. Wilczynski, The Economics of Socialism (London: Allen and Unwin, 1970), pp. 143-44.
4. John P. Morgan, "The Financial Aspects of East-West Trade," Columbia Journal of World Business 8 (Winter 1973): 53.
5. Jozef M. P. van Brabant, Essays on Planning in Eastern Europe (Rotterdam: Rotterdam University, 1974), pp. 12-13.
6. Wilczynski, Socialist Economic Development, op. cit., p. 288.
7. Kazimierz Grzbowski, "Organization and Conduct of Foreign Trade in Countries With State-Planned Economies: Comecon," in East-West Business Transactions, ed. Robert Starr (New York: Praeger, 1974), p. 129.
8. Henry Wilcox Schaefer, Comecon and the Politics of Integration (New York: Praeger, 1972), p. 101.
9. Brabant, op. cit., p. 13.
10. Ibid., pp. 94-96.
11. "The Investment Bank," East Europe 19 (November 1970): 45-46.
12. "The Advantages of An Investment Bank," East Europe 19 (November 1970): 42-43.
13. Ladislav Rusmich, "Financing The Investment Bank," (Interview) East Europe 20 (January 1971): 47-48.
14. Wolfgang Schmitz, "Monetary Dynamic Forces in East and West: Important Developments in the Seventies," in Convertibility, Multilateralism and Freedom, ed. Wolfgang Schmitz (New York: Springer, 1972), p.229.
15. Carl H. McMillan, Changing Perspective In East-West Commerce (Lexington: Heath, 1974), p. 143.
16. Ibid., p. 144.
17. Jay A. Burgess, "The Socialist Republic of Romania," in East-West Business Transactions, ed. Robert Starr (New York: Praeger, 1974), p. 282.

18. James A. Ramsey, "The 'Euroruble'—Competition or Convertibility?," Columbia Journal of World Business 3 (November-December 1968): 64.

19. Burgess, op. cit., p. 279.

20. McMillan, op. cit., p. 143.

21. Thomas W. Hoya, "Regulation of East-West Business Transactions by Market-Economy Countires: The United States," in East-West Business Transactions, ed. Robert Starr (New York: Praeger, 1974), p. 27.

22. Samuel Pisar, Coexistence and Commerce (New York: McGraw-Hill, 1970), p. 178.

23. Brabant, op. cit., pp. 263-64.

24. Wilczynski, Socialist Economic Development, op. cit., pp. 279-80.

25. Raymond F. Mikesell and Jack N. Behrman, Financing Free World Trade With the Sino-Soviet Bloc (Princeton: Princeton University, 1958), pp. 53-59.

26. Ibid., p. 97.

27. Robert W. Dean, West German Trade With the East: The Political Dimension (New York: Praeger, 1974), p. 14.

28. Jozef M. P. van Brabant, Bilateralism and Structural Bilateralism in Intra-CMEA Trade (Rotterdam: Rotterdam University, 1973), pp. 100-01.

29. Ibid., pp. 102-03.

30. Dean, op. cit., p. 5.

31. Wilczynski, Economics of Socialism, op. cit., pp. 42-43.

32. Adolf Hermann, "Can Comecon Integrate?," East Europe 18 (May 1969): 16.

33. Wilczynski, Socialist Economic Development, op. cit., p. 281.

PART

III

THE FINANCING OF FOREIGN TRADE

CHAPTER

6

EAST EUROPEAN CONSIDERATIONS CONCERNING CREDIT

The position of money and credit policy in the CMEA countries has been changing. Frankly, credit policy is a new phenomenon in the planned economies, because in the old systems there was no room for an autonomous role of money and credit.[1] Actually, export credits belong both to the field of trade policy, as an instrument for promoting exports, and to that of private financial activity. The field is a complex one, and one in which official, semiofficial and private action all play a part in creating and administering this type of finance.[2] We are primarily concerned with those aspects of credit which become instruments of trade policy by means of government intervention. First, we shall consider some general aspects of the Eastern European need for credit. Secondly, we shall try to assess the availability of credit in the industrialized West. Finally, we shall look at the policies of the U.S. government as they apply to credit for CMEA member countries.

GENERAL ASPECTS OF THE EAST EUROPEAN NEED FOR CREDIT

National Financing of Enterprises

In the past, the socialist countries have had virtually no capital market. Both providers and users of capital are socialized entities, and the three main sources of investment finance have been the state budget, banks, and the enterprises' own resources. Since the economic reforms, the role of direct state financing has declined in favor of bank credits; in the long run, this will lead to a much more effective and efficient use of resources. Although the total amount of credit and the proportions allowed to different branches are still centrally fixed according to the planned needs of the economy, microeconomic distribution is left to the judgment of the enterprises and the banks. Short-term credits are relatively unimportant in the CMEA compared with Western countries, and trade credits on commodity turnover are extended only by banks, not by the selling enterprises. Such short-term credit is strictly regulated because it could easily interfere with the planned utilization of resources. In extending long-term credit, emphasis is no longer on the sheer size of the projects, but rather on their suitability and efficiency. Preference is given to the projects which promise quick returns, which directly affect exports and import-replacement production, and which are intended for the less-developed regions.[3]

The shift from state budget financing to bank credit financing has been substantial, as indicated by Table 6.1.[4] With that change, there has been an increase in the general level and function of interest rates, which have become highly differentiated according to the purposes of credit; profitability has largely replaced need as the main criterion for credit extension. Still, the highly differentiated interest rates are not as much an ingenious device as they are a cumbersome method of compensating for the widely differing profitability of different enterprises as a consequence of the continued distortions in the price structures of the CMEA economies. In general, the effectiveness of the new interest rate systems under present socialist conditions has been exaggerated. Credits and interest rates cannot have a decisive influence on the distribution of resources, as they do in capitalist countries, since central planning determines the broad pattern of allocation of the factors of production. Rather, interest rates serve at best only a microeconomic function. Not to be overlooked also is the fact that the socialist countries, due to long neglect of banking and financing, lack a sufficiently qualified pool of personnel experienced in such matters.[5]

The case of Hungary offers a good example of the investment difficulties of the socialist countries. Chronic shortages of capital place tension on the investment market. The problem has been made much worse, however, by almost 20 years of extensive economic development during which scarce resources were spread impossibly thin. This has resulted in huge and continuing losses to the national economy due to numerous incomplete projects and delays. It has been estimated that Hungary requires two or two and one-half times as long as most Western nations to process and complete her investments.[6]

TABLE 6.1

Change in Percentage Proportion of Source of Finance
1963 and 1968

	Bulgaria		Hungary		Poland	
	1963	1968	1963	1968	1963	1968
Budgetary grants	70	43	75	49	48	28
Enterprises' own funds	29	31	24	39	44	52
Bank credits	1	26	1	12	8	20

Source: J. Wilczynski, Socialist Economic Development and Reforms (New York: Praeger, 1972), p. 162.

Intrabloc Credit

The International Bank for Economic Cooperation (IBEC) grants five kinds of credits for special purposes: overdrafts at 2.5 percent; seasonal credits expiring at the end of the current year for countries exporting agricultural produce; nonplanned credits, repayable at a higher rate of interest by the end of the year, for countries which lag behind in their plan targets; trade expansion credits of two-year terms to help overcome transitional disequilibria; and balance-of-payments credits in case of unforeseeable short-falls in export, such as poor crop yields due to bad weather, and which are to be repaid after a two-year terms.[7]

Before 1966, the limit of credits free of interest was 2.5 percent of the mutual trade; since then, a new agreement to ensure the profitability of the IBEC ruled that interest should be paid on one and one-half the amount of outstanding accounting and seasonal credits. To improve the credit system, it will be necessary to eliminate the present discrimination by credit types. Also, the terms of expiration should be made independent of the calendar years, and interest rates should be raised to an economically justifiable level and differentiated according to the terms of expiration.[8]

One of the basic shortcomings of the CMEA credit operations in the past has been their extending of mutual "credits for well-defined purposes." Such credits have usually formed an integral part of the long-term trade agreements and of the coordination of development plans in the CMEA. The direct reason for these far from negligible flows of capital among the Comecon countries stems from the chronic disequilibria on the CMEA market caused by the absence of built-in adjustment mechanisms of market forces. Furthermore, the problems have been greatly accelerated due to the recent efforts to attach efficiency considerations to trade and production, for such efforts have opened a pandora's box.

Theoretically, the advance of capital by the more advanced CMEA countries to those which are less developed would be desirable, since primary goods of the entire bloc could then be better utilized. However, the market horizon of such "credits for well-defined purposes" is artificially limited to the CMEA countries, and it might be more advantageous to extend the technological level of domestic industry and to import primary goods from nonsocialist countries. Also, the loans have been based on the capital-intensity of projects, which is really not a decisive criterion for allocating scarce investment funds. Finally, in addition to the loans being tied, this form of credit does not touch the bases of the unsatisfactory structure and the existing forms of intra-CMEA bilateralism. Complicating the picture is the fact that CMEA loans and repayments are transferred at relative prices which are different from relative prices in the borrower and the lender country, from world relative prices, and from terms of trade which are implied by the production conditions in the Comecon countries.[9]

Before the 1970 founding of the International Investment Bank (IIB), which specifically was to foster intrabloc integration through investments, the level of intrabloc loans was both low and one-sided. Table 6.2 shows the level of USSR credits to Eastern European countries between 1945 and 1969. It is quite noticeable that the USSR had concentrated on Bulgarian economic development more than on that of any other East European country, due presumably to the strategic importance of Bulgaria in the Soviet plans for the Mediterranean region, as well as to the fact that Bulgaria has the most abundant labor supply of all East European countries.[10] Such inequity is not unusual in intrabloc credit schemes, in which interest rates have operated heavily against the creditor. Thus Czechoslovakia, which pays 8 percent on suppliers' credit to West Germany and more to other Western countries, has in the past received no interest on its credit balance on the Soviet clearing account except after meeting special requirements.[11]

The fact still remains that convertibility of national currencies is the most important requisite for a successful functioning of the supraregional capital market. The IIB grants loans in convertible currencies only for the acquisition of necessary capital goods on the world market. The 70 percent capital subscriptions in transferable

TABLE 6.2

USSR Credits to Eastern Europe, 1945-69
(millions of U.S. dollars)

Country	Years	Credits
Albania	1957-1960	246.0
Bulgaria	1947-1969	1,800.0
Czechoslovakia	1947-1957	62.0
East Germany	1953-1962	1,701.2
Hungary	1954-1958	439.7
Poland	1947-1957	997.8
Romania	1947-1957	189.0
Total		5,435.7

Source: Richard F. Staar, The Communist Regimes in Eastern Europe (Stanford: Stanford University, 1971), p. 242.

rubles represent only an obligation to make deliveries up to the subscription amount of certain capital goods to a borrower as specified by the bank. Since the Comecon members at present have hardly any "convertible" capital goods at their disposal apart from trade obligations, the credit activity of the bank and the applications for credit to date have been extremely low, totaling not quite 2 percent of the present export volume on intrabloc trade.[12]

The CMEA Need for Credit

There are two primary sources of the need of the Comecon countries for credit. One is the shortage of convertible currencies and reserves, and the other is the emphasis on industrial development and rapid growth. The latter greatly affects the period in which finance is required, while in many cases of trading in consumer goods and raw materials, short-term finance is quite able to provide adequate facilities. On the other hand, sales of machinery and equipment on a credit basis generally require longer terms (from three to five years), and heavy capital equipment and complete plants often necessitate credit facilities on a basis of ten to fifteen years. The increasing share of capital equipment and machinery in the foreign trade of the CMEA has been reflected in the growing extension of medium- and long-term financing of East-West trade, a trend which is clearly predicted to continue.[13]

Not only the need for such credit hinders the expansion of trade, but the fact that the rates of interest which the CMEA countries are usually willing to pay are seldom in line with those currently existing on the international financial markets. In turn, this places the small- and medium-sized Western companies at a severe disadvantage. Actually, even the existence of long-term credit does not do much to expand East-West trade, for such trade is still kept at the level of the Eastern countries' abilities to balance their imports with exports. In other words, long-term credit is usually to be repaid only by supplies of future goods, so Western credits mean virtually the financing of future exports from Eastern bloc countries, for which a market must be found. In spite of such general patterns, however, an increasing use of hard currency to pay for Eastern imports has been noticed.[14]

There are several fundamental considerations which hold for all economies, including those of the CMEA. Economic growth can be created by importing more than exporting, and that is when international credit enters the picture. Such an increase in available resources can either be used for raising current consumption or be invested, the latter of which should, if successful, benefit future consumption. There is a definite cost in any event, that is, whether credit is obtained or not. Interest costs represent a commitment to transfer more real goods and services in the future, whereas the cost of not having credit is that of giving up goods for export to earn convertible foreign currencies. These basic rules do not tend to deemphasize the fact that CMEA trade has become increasingly more complex. In turn, the trend toward long-term, complicated engagements demands financing arrangements of matching complexity, and international financial institutions are needed to develop the sophisticated and flexible agreements.[15]

The question of credit is becoming increasingly important to the CMEA vis-a-vis the West, for five main reasons: CMEA deficits in East-West trade have grown much more rapidly than trade with these countries in the last decade and a half; the greater importance of Western capital goods requires longer-term financing; the continued growth of the Eastern economies requires not only more technology, but also the ability to purchase on the world market essential energy supplies, raw materials, and semimanufactures; their conventional exports are finding fewer and fewer markets; and their future commodity export potential is generally considered unfavorable.[16]

Another consideration of some importance in light of the East European need for credit is the fact that the CMEA countries, to promote trade with the developing countries, extend credits to such customers. Among the Eastern European countries, the export surplus in trade with the developing countries has been borne mainly by Czechoslovakia and to a lesser extent by Poland. During 1954-64, the CMEA countries extended about $6.4 billion in long-term economic aid to 33 developing countries, aid which has generally been in the form of low-interest credits.[17] Actually, the developing countries like such bilateral arrangements that are made with the Comecon nations. For one thing, the developing countries tend to be heavily dependent upon a few primary commodity exports for their foreign exchange earnings, and the instability of prices and demand in international markets has a severe impact on their internal economies, their foreign exchange reserves, and their development programs. The CMEA arrangements have offered them a stable market for their exports at favorable prices.[18] The 1972 trip of Ceausescu of Romania is illustrative of East-developing countries arrangements. He visited several African nations and granted to Egypt a $100 million credit to be used to finance Egyptian projects, at 3 to 4 percent, and tied the credit to purchases of Romanian goods. Quite simply, Romania needs to find new markets for its own expanding industry, as well as sources of raw materials.[19] Naturally, political considerations weighed quite heavily in the agreement.

CMEA POLICIES WITH RESPECT TO WESTERN CREDITS

In aggregate, East European demand for Western imports greatly exceeds the capacity to pay for them, which creates one of the principal bottlenecks in East-West trade. It has given rise to a chronic deficit on the Eastern side, as well as to continuing requests that Western governments increase the limits of indebtedness or extend to the CMEA countries outright middle- and long-term credits.[20] In the first half of 1975, the CMEA countries borrowed the equivalent of about $1.19 billion in the European market. Though that scale of borrowing is unprecendented, the bloc countries were, for the most part, able to negotiate better terms than most capitalist countries have obtained.[21] Most of the loans have been medium-term, and are general-purpose borrowing, as distinct from trade credits or financing for specific projects.

The borrowing flurry largely reflects the efforts of the CMEA countries to cover growing trade deficits with Western Europe, the United States, and Japan. Fortunately for the East Europeans, many Western banks are flush because of the recession, which has pushed savings rates high and depressed the domestic demand for money.

Part of the increased borrowing by the smaller members of Comecon has resulted from Moscow's demand that they pay for imports of Russian oil in hard currency. Another explanation is that two or three years ago, several East European nations agreed to supply oil and commodities to developing countries, with the intent of building up political capital by buying the raw materials on the world market, then selling them on favorable terms. However, world prices have soared, and the East European countries now must borrow hard cash to finance their now costly commitments. All in all, the Eastern banks' position vis-a-vis Eurobanks rose from $5 billion at the end of 1974 to over $7.5 billion by April 1975, and is undoubtedly higher now. Several countries, including Romania and Bulgaria, are approaching the upper limits of debt, as has Poland in regard to Germany, with whom it has a $800 million trade deficit.[22]

The debt-service ratio of the Eastern bloc countries, excluding the USSR, is unusually high. While all the smaller members prefer a product payback credit arrangement, such transactions are really only feasible when the loan is extended for natural resource development projects, rather than the industrial projects which the CMEA members emphasize. We have already noted that only recently have the smaller CMEA countries sought new sources of capital through commercial banks in the West. In general, all of the countries under consideration acknowledge the importance of Western credits, but as we shall see, the policies of CMEA countries with respect to Western credits differ from one another, a fact which is partly a reflection of the availability of credits and partly a consequence of each CMEA country's special economic conditions, the attitude of its political leadership, and the extent of Soviet backing with hard-currency loans and guarantees.[23]

Bulgaria. Western credit represents an important growth factor for Bulgaria. However, Bulgaria has not systematically sought credits, and turns to the West only sporadically, perhaps when additional imports were necessary to fulfill five-year plans. We have already noted, however, that Bulgaria has been particularly favored by the USSR in regard to credits, so that perhaps the fluctuations of Bulgaria's credit from the West reflect Soviet policies as well as her own.[24]

Czechoslovakia. Among all CMEA countries, Czechoslovakia has made the least use of foreign credits in financing its foreign trade and internal development. Until recently, many Czechoslovak purchases in the West were made on a cash basis, with little attempt to secure medium- or long-term credit. Recently, however, there have been indications that this policy is changing, perhaps in response to climbing world prices for manufactures and commodities, and it is anticipated that the availability of credits will be an increasingly important factor in Czechoslovak foreign trade policy.[25]

East Germany. Because of its political and economic isolation, East Germany has had fewer policy options with respect to Western credits than perhaps any other CMEA country. However, its relationship with West Germany, as we shall see, has been the major source of Western credit, and of substantial significance. Moreover, as indicated in Table 6.2, East Germany, like Bulgaria, has had favorable treatment from the USSR in financing its deficit with the West.

Hungary. There was a significant shift in Hungarian policy toward Western credit in the second half of 1974. Whereas Hungary had traditionally pursued a conservative and selective borrowing policy, the seeking out of foreign credits has been noticeably increased.[26] In addition, in May 1971, she became the first CMEA country to float a bond issue on the international Eurodollar market.[27] A more recent floating of Hungary, in 1975, received very poor reception in West Germany, due largely to the fact that Hungary is a communist country.[28]

Poland. Political attitudes have been the major determinant of Poland's policy with respect to Western credits. Wladyslaw Gomulka, the former leader, was firmly convinced that Poland's East-West trade should be carefully balanced, and often adjustments were made by slashing of purchases essential to the economy. To the extent that hard-currency credits were absolutely necessary, Gomulka favored short- and medium-term credits rather than long-term credits. In 1971, the new Polish leader, Edward Gierek, reversed both aspects of Gomulka's conservative policy. He accepted large deficits and credits to import consumer goods and also to finance new investments to modernize the economy. As a consequence, Poland's trade deficit with the West in 1971, 1972, and 1973 amounted to around $300, $500, and $800 million, respectively. Poland's hard-currency debt is now estimated at some $3 billion, and its total debt-service payments to all its creditors, both East and West, are estimated at 13.2 percent of national income at the end of 1973. The country is still seeking large, long-term loans from Western countries, and promises large purchases from countries willing to provide such credits.[29] In 1975, the Poles borrowed $50 million a week to help make up an estimated $2 billion trade deficit.[30] Early in 1975, the Poles received a $240 million loan from a consortium led by Chase Manhattan Bank,[31] and in addition to that received a huge $1.6 billion credit from France, with payments not due until the financed projects are producing, a condition which France accepted as means of paving the road for further joint projects.[32]

Romania. As in the case of Bulgaria, credits represent an extremely important growth factor for Romania. The ratio of hard-currency debt to hard-currency exports for Romania is the highest in the CMEA, and in fact twice that of Bulgaria, which has the second highest ratio. Thus, the contribution of Western loans to its economy, as well as the relative burden of financing the debt, is extremely high for Romania. Much of this is due to the Romanian policies of independence in the CMEA, a course which it has pursued since the early 1960s. At that time, the country was able to reorient its trade patterns from the CMEA to the West, at least to a substantial degree. By 1973, the Romanian debt (hard-currency) stood at $2 billion, and, in contrast to Bulgaria, it had little or no financial backing from Russia. Today, Romania is still confidently and heroically trying to service the debt while maintaining its rapid rate of industrial growth. It has joined the International Monetary Fund, has established banks in Paris and London, and as we shall see later, intends to expand its economic ties with the West.[33]

In 1975 the indebtedness of Comecon to the West jumped 42 percent to $32 billion.[34] In general, then, we have seen that, on the Eastern side, regardless of level of development, all countries under consideration exhibit a strong demand for Western credits. This is indicated not only by their level of indebtedness, but by their active search for new sources of credit. Still, there is considerable difference among these countries as to the role which foreign credit plays. An overriding issue of the near future will be the ability of the countries to service their debts as well as to find new sources or expand old ones. We shall now consider the problem from the other side, that is, we shall look at the capital markets in the West and try to determine their position in regard to East-West credit patterns.

NOTES

1. Wolfgang Schmitz, "Monetary Dynamic Forces in East and West: Important Developments in the Seventies," in Convertibility, Multilateralism and Freedom, ed. Wolfgang Schmitz (New York: Springer, 1972), p. 237.

2. Organization for Economic Cooperation and Development, Trade Measures and Adjustment of the Balance of Payments (Paris: OECD, 1971), p. 57.

3. J. Wilczynski, The Economics of Socialism (London: Allen and Unwin, 1970), pp. 146-47.

4. J. Wilczynski, Socialist Economic Development and Reforms (New York: Praeger, 1972), p. 162.

5. Ibid., pp. 152-58.

6. William F. Robinson, The Pattern of Reform in Hungary: A Political, Economic and Cultural Analysis (New York: Praeger, 1973), pp. 157-58.

7. Bela Csikos-Nagy, Socialist Economic Policy (New York: St. Martin's, 1973), p. 221.

8. Sandor Ausch, Theory and Practice of CMEA Cooperation (Budapest: Academiai Kiado, 1972), p. 264.

9. Jozef M. P. van Brabant, Essays on Planning in Eastern Europe (Rotterdam: Rotterdam University, 1974), pp. 175-80, 189.

10. Bogoslav Dobrin, Bulgarian Economic Development Since World War II (New York: Praeger, 1973), p. 147.

11. Adolf Hermann, "Can Comecon Integrate?," East Europe 18 (May 1969): 17.

12. Heinrich Machowski, "Toward A Socialist Economic Integration of Eastern Europe," in Eastern Europe in the 1970s, ed. Sylva Sinanian, Istvan Deak, and Peter C. Ludz (New York: Praeger, 1972), p. 196.

13. Nikolai V. Nikitkin, "Financing East-West Transactions—Use of United Kingdom-Based Institutions," in Financing East-West Business Transactions (New York: American Management Association, 1968), p. 17.

14. James R. Basche, Jr., East-West Trade: The Lessons From Experience (New York: Conference Board, 1971), pp. 22-23.

15. Gunter Dufey, "Financing East-West Business," Columbia Journal of World Business 9 (Spring 1974): 37, 39.

16. Carl H. McMillan, Changing Perspectives In East-West Commerce (Lexington: Heath, 1974), pp. 125-26.

17. Carole A. Sawyer, Communist Trade With Developing Countries: 1955-65 (New York: Praeger, 1966), pp. 22, 48.

18. Raymond F. Mikesell and Jack N. Behrman, Financing Free World Trade With the Sino-Soviet Bloc (Princeton: Princeton University, 1958), p. 17.

19. "Current Developments: Romania," East Europe 21 (June 1972): 44-47.

20. Robert W. Dean, West German Trade With the East: The Political Dimension (New York: Praeger, 1974), pp. 15-16.

21. "Communist Bloc Loans In Europe Seen Rising In 2nd Half From 1st," Wall Street Journal, October 16, 1975, p. 28.

22. "Eastern Europe: The East Bloc Looks Westward for Loans," Business Week 2399 (September 22, 1975): 38-39.

23. McMillan, op. cit., pp. 130-32.

24. Ibid., p. 132.

25. "Czechoslovakia Eyes Western Sources For Up-to-Date Technology, Equipment," Commerce Today 4 (April 15, 1974): 31.

26. U.S. Department of Commerce, "Hungary," Foreign Economic Trends ET 74-072 (August 1974): 8.

27. Robinson, op. cit., p. 160.

28. "The East Bloc Looks Westward," op. cit., pp. 38-39.

29. McMillan, op, cit., pp. 132-33.

30. "The East Bloc Looks Westward," op. cit., p. 38.

31. "Poland: Copper Major," The Economist 255 (June 28, 1975): 95-96.

32. "Polen und Frankreich demonstrieren 'privilegierte Beziehungen,'" Frankfurter Allgemeine Zeitung, June 18, 1975, p. 4.

33. McMillan, op. cit., p. 132.

34. "The Debt That Overhangs East-West Dealings," Business Week 2430 (May 3, 1976): 118.

CHAPTER

7

WESTERN CREDIT AND EAST-WEST TRADE

OFFICIAL WESTERN CREDIT POLICIES

As well as Eastern orientation towards the West, the orientation of the West towards the East is of decisive importance to the availability of credit, which in turn is of the utmost importance for Eastern European purchases in the West. To extend the comparison, the availability of credit reflects not only economic factors but also differences among Western countries in their political posture toward East Europe (making West Germany a large creditor) and differences in political attitudes toward individual East European countries, a fact which has led to extensive credit availability for Romania. Because much of Western credit is granted under government guarantee, government policy is a decisive factor. In regard to the economics of credit availability, the composition of Western exports (primarily requiring medium- and long-term credit), the stage of the Western business cycle (credits are granted more readily for capital goods during slack periods), and the competition among Western countries to grant credits (to put their enterprises in a better competitive position) are important. In general, during the postwar period the credit policies of the Western countries have changed considerably from policies that reflected no interest whatsoever in extending credit to the CMEA to ones that actively encourage intense competition among Western countries, leading to subsidized credits to stimulate exports or to gain political concessions from the Eastern partner. More recently, there have been cooperative agreements among Western countries to regulate voluntarily the terms and interest structure of such credits.[1]

In early 1974, an agreement was reached by West European countries, in principle, not to extend long-term credit to communist countries for more than eight and a half years or at interest rates below 7 percent. Since that time, the U.S. Treasury and the Common Market Commission have held talks to establish more uniformity of credit policies. The sentiment seems to be for a "gentlemen's agreement" that Western countries should limit government-backed export credits to five years for rich Western countries, eight and a half years for the European CMEA countries, and ten years for the developing countries, with a 7 percent minimum interest rate.[2]

As early as 1934 the Berne Union was founded to which belonged the majority of export-credit institutions in Western countries and which endeavored to regulate the use of state-guaranteed credits. The objective was to prevent state guarantee of export credits from becoming a means for subsidizing exports and distorting the pattern of international trade based on relative costs. Over thirty years later, the Organization for Economic Cooperation and Development (OECD) still found it necessary to recommend that the governments of the Western countries reach an understanding to regulate the terms of credits that may be given to the East, whether direct government credit, government-guaranteed credit, or private credit. Like the Berne Union before, it believed that there should be a five-year limit to the duration of credits with no exceptions.[3] The recommendation, like that of the Berne Agreement before it, has proved to be largely ineffective, probably because Western Europe's trade relationship with East Europe has been built on credit. It started some years ago averaging three years, leveled off for a while at five, and by 1970 was averaging between eight and ten years, with the average cost being 5.5 percent.[4]

The failure of the Berne Union Agreement is due to a number of circumstances. For one thing, its policy-making role was obscure; there is no formal international treaty, nor have the national parliaments given it legal approval. It did, however, serve two functions: it set standards for the granting of international credit, and it performed as an international information service, through which member states could verify exactly what credits had been made available to the bloc states. Its obvious intent was to prevent credit wars from developing in competition among its member nations.[5] More recently, the European Economic Community (EEC) has been trying to solve the problem through a policy-coordinating group for credit insurance, guarantees, and financial credits. A consultation procedure in such matters has been worked out, as amended by a council decision of December 3, 1973. Under the agreement, export credits and export credit guarantees granted by member states or by institutions acting for the member states are subject to prior notification of other member states and the commission, if they are linked to the export of products or services of the member states concerned and have a duration of more than five years, or if they depart from any other common norm adopted by the Community, irrespective of whether the source of the funds is public or private. Common credit policies for medium- and long-term transactions have been adopted by the EEC, but they are not yet in force.[6]

Breaches of such agreements have been fairly common in the past. They have, in general, not covered state direct loans, and only recently have they included private credits. There are several factors which tend to make a more effective limit on credit to the East necessary. First, it has already been made clear that the CMEA countries are actively and aggressively seeking a substantial increase of credit from the West. Second, because it is the Eastern state which is a party on one side, the Western government is also almost always involved, whatever the nominal form of the credit. In such a situation, normal market forces are not permitted to exert their full influence on the arrangements. Because governments are involved on both sides, the extension of credit on terms exceeding commercial practice takes on political significance.[7] In spite of the general agreement that such limitations on credit are essential, the United States, Japan and the EEC were still meeting in 1975 trying to hammer out an acceptable agreement. The issue took on additional significance since all the industrialized countries were faced with deteriorating balance-of-payments positions. The main agenda items were the lengths for which credits should be granted, and what the minimum interest rates should be. However, as pointed out in The Economist:

> "But the flesh is weak, the balance-of-trade figures menace, and one export credit institution after another is pushed by its exporters, its customers or its government to lend for longer, to lend cheaper, to counteract domestic inflation or whatever else may safeguard jobs and prettify the balance-of-trade statistics."[8]

Complicating the decisions of Western governments as to their credit policies towards the CMEA countries is the lack of reliable statistical information concerning CMEA balance of payments and the future prospects of the CMEA countries for hard-currency earnings. Additionally, the credit patterns which emerge contain aspects which are realized under capitalist conditions and are governed by capitalist laws and principles, yet; they include other aspects which make themselves manifest under the conditions of a socialist economy. Generally the socialist nations have no desire to encroach upon the economic independence of Western countries,[9] although the same cannot be said for Western countries.

Western European countries have traditionally used numerous tactics to encourage exports through credit facilities. Advances to enable exporters to offer their customers longer credit terms were made by the central banks or by official institutions set up specially for the purpose. Another common form of government aid is the arranging or providing of insurance or guarantees against the risks attaching to exports. A third type of government intervention has been the influencing of the terms of credit by a series of measures tending to reduce costs. All of these measures include an element of subsidy which must, in the last resort, be financed out of the state budget. Gradually, there has been an erosion of the earlier conservative standards of credit, an evolution which is directly fostered by the competitiveness on export markets. It is widely recognized that such government policies do not affect the balance of payments rapidly, since most of the export credits granted are for medium- or long-term. Thus the immediate effects are negative since they affect the capital account of the balance of payments. Whatever the case, any easing of the terms of credit is a source of both internal and external distortion, and if the modifications are only marginal, their effect is probably quite small. If the modifications are significant, their effect is surely to be minimized since other countries will follow suit, so that, in general, the effectiveness of increased export credit facilities as a means of correcting balance-of-payments deficits seems doubtful.[10]

West Germany and Great Britain have been the largest trading partners of the Western world with the CMEA countries. Accordingly, it would be advantageous to consider their policies in respect to credits. As we shall see, West Germany has a much more politically oriented policy, whereas the United Kingdom has one which is primarily economically oriented. Quite naturally, that stems from the political and economic strengths and weaknesses of each country.

To West Germany, the problem of East-West trade is political. In terms of volume, the trade flow between East and West Germany has been the single most important bilateral commercial exchange in East-West trade, and it is inseparable from the political issues that divide the two Germanys. West Germany considers the trade between these two nations as domestic trade, whereas the East Germans consider it as foreign trade. The trade itself has been used as cement for integration and reunification purposes, and to gain all kinds of political concessions, in which the West Germans have been consistently outmaneuvered by the East Germans. At the same time, the

Ostpolitik of Willy Brandt and now Helmut Schmidt represents an about-face from the Ostpolitik of Konrad Adenauer, so that a definite evolution of policies has been noticeable. The political nature of the East German policies is noted by the fact that not until the USSR became unwilling to further underwrite East German development did the German Democratic Republic (GDR) turn to West Germany for extensive credit.[11]

The predominantly political significance of Eastern trade to West Germany has deeply affected the Federal Republic of Germany (FRG) regulatory scheme with respect to such trade. Officially taboo, such trade still has not found its way into any legal provisions of West Germany, and only recently, under the inspiration of Brandt, could such trade be freely mentioned in most circles. Once the limitation of West German trade with the GDR was set at a total debit balance on either side of the bilateral relationship to 200 million units of account; however, in 1968 the annual balancing obligation was abolished with an agreement expiring in 1975, so that no balancing has taken place since then. A "commercialization" of the swing suggested by West German trade representatives, through an interim solution that would accustom the GDR slowly to the payment of interest, has not yet reached the stage of realization. Interestingly, the normal credit institutions of West Germany, such as Hermes, cannot guarantee credit between the two Germanys since such trade is not considered by the West Germans to be foreign trade.[12] Many other considerations must be taken into account in determining credit between these two countries, because of their unique relationship. Between 1970 and 1974, for example, West Germany paid to East Germany over 2.8 billion marks simply for transit costs.[13]

Compared to its relationship with East Germany, West Germany's relationship with the other CMEA members is not quite so complicated. Still, Poland's case underlines again the strongly political orientation of West German foreign trade. In August 1975, Germany gave credit to Poland of over 2.3 billion marks at a low 2.5 percent interest, with a 25-year term. The purpose of the credit, primarily, was to solve certain important (political) questions in the relationship of the two countries.[14] The actual issue revolves around resettlement of Polish citizens who are of German descent. In spite of the favorable terms, it is anticipated that Gierek will have difficulty with the Poles, who are skeptical of German political aims.[15] Schmidt is having trouble with the Germans, for the parliament does not like the terms of the agreement.[16] The British maintain that "having accepted the unpalatable principle of trading humanitarian gains against hard cash, Germany is not pretending to have got much of a bargain."[17] Nevertheless, such is the nature of German credit to the East bloc.

On the Eastern side, all CMEA members with the exception of Romania issued their terms, separately, for the normalization of relations with West Germany: recognition of existing borders, West German recognition of the GDR, and the renunciation of atomic weapons. Romania at the time was making overtures to the West, and it is ironic that its troubles with West Germany concerning credit have been of a primarily economic measure. The Romanians were forced to demand that German exporters undertake to secure West German imports of their goods to at least 50 percent of the value of any individual West German export transaction, a demand made even more complicated since West Germany has to also satisfy Common Market import regulations. Interestingly, West Germany's relationships with Czechoslovakia have also been relatively free of political objectives. In what perhaps reflects a new change of policy around 1970, Economics Minister Karl Schiller said, "Export guarantees are an instrument of export stimulus, not a political declaration of love."[18] Notwithstanding that comment, credit policy in Germany has a long way to go before it is free of political orientation.

The British credit policy is primarily economically oriented. The Export Credit and Guarantee Department offers substantial incentives for both suppliers' credit and buyers' credit, through which the foreign buyer or his bank obtains a loan from a British bank at a special low export finance rate.[19] In addition, the clearing banks and merchant banks participate widely in East-West trade, and U.K. insurance companies provide insurance for international trade. It was the Moscov Narodny Bank Ltd. of London that was the first to engage actively in the finance of East-West trade on a large scale and on a long-term basis.[20] It was also England which organized the first consortium loan for the CMEA, in 1972.[21] Several factors stimulate such developments in the United Kingdom. The pound is sinking, making prices for goods lower relatively in Great Britain than elsewhere in Europe. Also, many of the CMEA countries have large deficits with West Germany, and for that reason are more or less forced to look towards Great Britain. Also not to be overlooked is the fact that the United Kingdom offers particularly low-interest export credits to communist trade partners.[22]

In fact, with the exception of the United States, all Western industrialized countries provide relatively greater credit support for East-West trade than for their overall trade. This is explained in part by greater interest rate sensitivities in the socialist countries and also by their foreign trade monopoly power.[23] However, the main rationales seem to be: inherently greater credit needs of the socialist countries; greater perceptions of commercial and political risks by Western exporters; higher capital goods intensity of exports; and Western foreign policy considerations.[24] Still, it was not until the early 1960s that the availability of Western European Government-assisted credits allowed East Europe to import machinery and equipment at a rate faster than their hard-currency export earnings could otherwise support. In the 1960-70 period, the CMEA borrowed Western government-guaranteed credits amounting to approximately $5.5 to $6 billion, in addition to substantial amounts of uninsured private credits. Together with increasing East European hard-currency indebtedness, this led to the situation in which credit terms increasingly became the focal point in trade negotiations.[25]

OFFICIAL CREDIT POLICIES OF THE UNITED STATES

It was not until the 1970s that the United States seriously considered entering the export credit race to serve the East European countries. By the early 1970s, this country's bilateral relations with Poland, Romania, and the USSR had progressed to the point where Eximbank credits could be offered under Presidential determinations that it was in the national interest to do so. Such a development is of tremendous importance to the East European countries, for the United States represents (with the exception of the Arab oil exporting countries) East Europe's last major untapped source of long-term hard-currency credit.[26]

There can be no question that U.S. trade with the CMEA has been at a distinct competitive disadvantage due to our export credit policies. The effect has often been that American companies have been forced to deliver manufactured components of their successful contracts from third countries where they can obtain government-sponsored credit.[27] Quite obviously, the future of U.S.-CMEA trade depends much on what happens in the United States Congress. President Ford has recently indicated to the congressmen the need to modify those provisions in the Trade Act of 1974 that link extension of most favored nation (MFN) and Eximbank credits to emigration policies of the socialist countries. If the Congress responds favorably, the path will be cleared to increased trade. If no action is taken, it is anticipated that U.S. trade will continue to grow with Poland and Romania, but that such trade would probably stagnate around its present levels with Bulgaria, Czechoslovakia, East Germany, and Hungary.[28] Clearly, the U.S. export policy has been a serious obstacle to U.S. exports. It is, in fact, estimated that since 1960, U.S. com-

TABLE 7.1

U.S. Trade With the CMEA Countries Under Consideration, 1969-74
(thousands of dollars)

	1969	1970	1971	1972	1973	1974
U.S. Exports						
Bulgaria	4,645	15,294	4,353	3,543	6,474	18,100
Czechoslovakia	14,363	22,512	38,726	49,993	72,050	35,200
East Germany	32,373	32,545	25,441	17,473	28,025	19,000
Hungary	7,252	28,263	27,873	22,613	32,956	49,500
Poland	52,694	69,915	73,271	113,642	349,993	318,900
Romania	32,394	66,399	52,532	69,428	116,614	218,200
U.S. Imports						
Bulgaria	5,598	2,431	2,614	2,872	4,458	7,700
Czechoslovakia	24,063	23,892	23,597	27,972	35,154	38,000
East Germany	8,018	9,394	10,136	10,336	10,515	12,200
Hungary	4,077	6,224	7,751	12,725	16,420	67,700
Poland	97,835	97,946	107,641	139,172	181,904	216,400
Romania	7,966	13,425	13,774	31,487	55,704	112,200

Source: 1969-73 figures from: United States Department of Commerce, "Trade of the United States With Socialist Countries in Eastern Europe and Asia, 1971-73," *Overseas Business Reports*, OBR 74-24 (June 1974), p. 1. 1974 figures represent only the first 10 months of that year, and stem from: United States Department of Commerce, "World Trade Outlook For Eastern Europe, Union of Soviet Socialist Republics and People's Republic of China," *Overseas Business Reports*, OBR 75-19, (March 1975), p. 2.

panies have exported at least three times more machinery and equipment to Eastern Europe through affiliates in Europe than from plants in this country, part of the reason for which is simply the unavailability of medium- and long-term credit in this country.[29] The relatively low level of U.S. trade with Comecon is noted in Table 7.1. Consequently, we should give consideration to official U.S. policy in this area.

The Johnson Act of 1934

The subsidization of U.S. credits to CMEA members has been restricted by the Johnson Act of 1934, which prohibits certain private financial transactions involving governments which are in payment default to the United States, unless they are members of the International Monetary Fund (IMF) or the World Bank. However, although the Act affects loans to most CMEA countries because of their outstanding debts contracted before the socialist regimes took power, for which they do not recognize responsibility, the Attorney General has ruled that the Act does not prohibit export financing arrangements if they are directly tied to specific export transactions. Accordingly, this interpretation exempts loans with Eximbank participation.[30]

With the exceptions of Albania and Bulgaria, all of the European CMEA countries are considered to be in default under the Johnson Act, which stems primarily from World War I debts and lend-lease. At present, the major purpose of the Act seems to be the political one of denying the communist nations medium- and long-term nongovernmental credits, for their share of such debts is less than 4 percent, and the exemption of Western European nations has been made on the basis of membership in organizations quite unrelated to their debt defaults and to the original concept of the Johnson Act.[31] Exemptions from the Johnson Act have been granted to Romania, since it is now a member of the IMF and the International Bank for Reconstruction and Development.[32] All in all, the Act does not cover extensions of normal commercial credit as part of a specific export transaction, but is directed at purely financial general purpose loans, a distinction which is not always easy to determine.

Credit Programs for the Encouragement of Agricultural Exports

The U.S. government promotes the export of agricultural products through three major programs: the Commodity Credit

Corporation's (CCC) Export Payment Programs, the CCC's Export Credit Sales Program, and PL 480. The first two programs do not discriminate against communist countries as such, whereas PL 480 does. Under the first program, the government pays the difference to the U.S. exporter when domestic prices of a certain agricultural commodity are higher than the world prices. Under the second, the government extends credit up to three years to U.S. exporters to assist them in selling abroad. Under 480, agricultural commodities are sold to friendly, that is, among other things, noncommunist, countries on long-term credit up to 20 years. This last program, however, does not severely affect East-West trade because of the presence of the other two programs. The actual impediment to such trade was the Kennedy Shipping Act, which was terminated by President Nixon in June 1971.[33] Even so, an exemption was made in the case of PL 480 for Poland for the specific purpose of rewarding or encouraging polycentric movements within the communist world.[34]

Although the CCC programs do not discriminate against the CMEA, they do not seem to actively foster a great deal of competition with the Western European programs. The commodity eligibility lists do not include goods if their export would put a strain on domestic stocks or if the importing country is self-sufficient in the commodity under consideration. Furthermore, the CCC credit interest rates are in line with commercial U.S. interest rates; the rates are not lowered when those of the banks in the importing country are low relative to U.S. rates. However, the CCC does take into consideration the overall competitiveness of its rates relative to other country suppliers of the eligible commodities. Generally, the ineffectiveness of the programs in stimulating trade has been due to the fact that the programs have been initiated in an attempt to lower the level of U.S. surplus agricultural commodities, rather than as a foreign policy ploy; that is, domestic considerations have dominated. Although the programs have been available to the CMEA countries since 1966 on a nondiscriminatory basis, use of them has been relatively low, a result not only of the factors which we have mentioned before, but also of weather and harvest patterns, current bilateral trade agreements, MFN status, hard-currency situations, and political considerations.[35]

The Eximbank

Ironically, the Eximbank was created in 1934 to help finance trade with the USSR. Its primary mission has changed several times during the course of its existence, and its major goal now is to help improve the U.S. balance of payments through export promotion. On June 30, 1974, the bank's charter required renewal by Congress, but it was far from routine, for many critics of the bank had appeared in the meantime, maintaining that the floating dollar made subsidization of export financing unnecessary, that the bank created competitive industrialization abroad, and that the bank was being used for uncertain political ends. However, the charter has been renewed until June 30, 1978, and its overall commitment authority was increased from $20 to $25 billion.[36] It is of particular importance to East-West trade, since there are substantial differences in exporting to East Europe as compared to the exporting to the rest of the world, due to the unique nature of East European economic activity under centralized political control.[37] On the other hand, it has been contended that the activities of the Eximbank distort the operations of private capital markets by setting a higher priority on financing export loans than on domestic loans in general. Still, in spite of assumed bad economics, it is often considered worthwhile to subordinate bad economics to good politics.[38]

Actually, Eximbank credit support for U.S. exports to socialist countries was negligible prior to 1964, when Congress encouraged such activity. Under the "national interest" provision, President Johnson issued four determinations permitting Eximbank support of exports of all "peaceful" products to Bulgaria, Czechoslovakia, Hungary, Poland, and Romania.[39] In 1968, however, Congress prohibited the bank from making any loans to any country assisting North Vietnam, and all of the countries under consideration in this book were included in that group. There was no discretion vested in the President to waive this absolute prohibition, and not until Congress repealed the prohibition in 1971 was the President again in a position to permit the bank to extend credits to members of the CMEA.[40] Currently, only the USSR, Romania, Poland and Yugoslavia are eligible for Eximbank credits among all socialist nations, and the President must determine that loans for $50 million or more to any socialist country would be in the national interest.[41]

It is clear that the Export-Import Bank Amendments of 1974, which reflected new perceptions of the relationship between economic and political gains, are a result primarily of the political goal of detente, and that U.S.-USSR relations are the dominant concern. The premise of the 1974 Amendment was that economic policy is an important tool in international relations, to be used flexibly and realistically for the achievement of economic and political objectives.[42] In the middle of concern over the growing interest in detente with the USSR, economic factors began to be taken more and more into consideration, since the United States was at the time caught in the middle of recession, inflation, and a growing oil shortage and energy crisis. The outcome of the legislation is essentially increased powers of the U.S. Congress in shaping our foreign trade, particularly with the Eastern bloc. Ceilings and subceilings were set, each of which is intended to provide an opportunity for Congressional participation in major policy decisions; furthermore, the Act requires the bank to notify the Congress 25 days before approval of any proposed loan, guarantee, or combination thereof in the amount of $60 million or more.[43]

The ceilings affect only Eximbank's direct loan program, not its commercial bank guarantee. Such loans have consistently followed a 10-45-45 pattern, in which the bank makes a loan from its own funds for 45 percent of the U.S. export costs, provided that a 10 percent down payment is made in each case and that the financing for the remaining 45 percent is obtained from outside sources. The interest rate charged on Eximbank's own funds is currently 7 percent, which, when blended with the outside financing, results in a combined rate of approximately 8.6 percent. By comparison, interest rates on the private market range around 12.5 percent. For fiscal year 1974, the ceiling on loan authorizations was set at $3.8 billion, which required the deferral of up to $1 billion in export loans until fiscal year 1975. In face of the new ceilings, Eximbank is presently considering various alternatives to its present financing pattern. One alternative would be to deny from 25 to 40 percent of the loan applications the bank otherwise would have approved. A second option would be to reduce Eximbank's support for certain export products which today account for a large proportion of Eximbank's total loan authorization. A third alternative would be to reduce the bank's participation in loans from the present 45 percent to a lower level, which would increase the cost to foreign buyers and possibly render U.S. exports less competitive.[44]

In the past few years, the U.S. government has been actively pursuing the expansion of trade with the CMEA countries. Of all its activities, however, Eximbank is the only government agency that has an active role in individual transactions, whereas other government activities have a more generalized impact. For this reason, if the U.S. government has a role to play in influencing East-West trade policy, which it most certainly does, the Eximbank's programs might well represent the most useful bargaining tool that the government has.[45]

FORMS OF EAST-WEST AGREEMENTS AT THE ENTERPRISE LEVEL

We have already briefly referred to the patterns, commodity structure, and government credit programs of East-West trade. The forces of bilateralism and inconvertibility, however, have affected East-West trade in other ways also. Accordingly, we turn now to the types of arrangements which have been either necessitated or preferred.

Although numerous recent agreements between governments have improved the climate for East-West trade, the real effects of mutual economic cooperation are realized through the interaction of individual enterprises, usually multinational corporations (MNCs), with the CMEA bodies. MNCs, in fact, carry out the highest percentage of East-West trade, and are basically well accepted by the CMEA states for three reasons: as a result of their advanced research abilities, they generally offer the socialist countries the most modern products and technology; MNCs are more able to undertake large contracts due to their greater output capacity; and since MNCs pursue global activities, they can adapt themselves more readily to changing conditions, particularly since they are less subject to governmental economic regulation than smaller enterprises oriented toward the home market.[46] The objective of this section is to reveal the nature of the agreements which they conclude with the Eastern bloc countries. For the most part, the advantages and disadvantages of the following forms of agreements are well known. As a result, emphasis shall be placed on those aspects which are most significant to East-West trade as such, instead of to trade in general.

Direct Investment in Socialist Countries and Cooperative Agreements

In Bulgaria, one of the most conservative of the CMEA countries, direct foreign investment remains illegal, and there is little likelihood that this will soon change. In fact, Western firms are not even allowed to station representatives in the country.[47] "Cooperation" to the Bulgarians does not mean joint ownership; rather, it implies a foreign firm's supplying technology and equipment which will lead to increased Bulgarian exports. In return, Bulgaria normally provides to the supplier a portion of the goods produced under the arrangement. Nevertheless, joint equity ventures in third countries are encouraged.[48] The same holds true for Czechoslovakia.[49] In

East Germany, joint equity ownership is also forbidden. However, in 1975 it began to open its eyes to joint projects with West Germany, in which payment to the West Germans would be out of the new production. The decisive factor in the change of attitude seems to stem from the East German need to increase its exports to be able to pay for the now much more expensive Russian oil.[50]

Joint equity venture agreements are possible, however, in Poland, Romania, and Hungary. While Poland has already concluded more than 50 such agreements with Western firms, it lags behind Romania and Hungary in such. Its slow progress in this area stems from the belief that the domestic system of prices, exchange rates, financial accounting, and plant management must undergo significant changes if such ventures are to be successful.[51] Hungary had prohibited shared equity arrangements until 1970, previous to which cooperation was limited to co-production schemes and licensing and training arrangements. However, as of mid-1974, the joint companies which the Hungarians have formed with Western firms have been located outside of Hungary. Still, the official decrees permit economic associations in the form of joint stock companies, share companies, limited liability companies or joint enterprises, in which "in general" the share of the foreign partner should not exceed 49 percent.[52] Romania was the first of the Comecon nations to pass legislation providing for non-Romanian firms to establish commercial offices and to make direct capital investment (again, up to 49 percent) in production enterprises in Romania, which provided a unique opening to Western firms interested in initiating or expanding their East-West trade business.[53] The U.S. government responded by authorizing Overseas Private Investment Corporation (OPIC) programs in Romania if the President determines it to be in the national interest. The President did so in March 1972, and now OPIC loan guarantee and investment insurance programs are available.[54]

Industrial cooperation has the following advantages for the CMEA countries: it permits close commercial contacts with a Western partner; it facilitates access to modern technology without additional costs; the CMEA countries are able to establish and develop commercial relations with the other countries in which subsidiaries of a Western partner operate; and it clearly may give rise to more sophisticated forms of economic cooperation in the future. However, there are also disadvantages of such forms of cooperation: in spite of easier access to the capitalist markets, the impact of the socialist producers is hardly noticeable, since Western trademarks are generally used, and this limits the socialist exporter's expansion possibilities; many of the cooperation plans take the form of one-way subcontracting, where the degree of profitability of multicomponent products is greatest at the end product stage, so that the only real gain for the socialist country is in technological expertise; finally, one consequence is that the socialist countries become dependent upon the business cycle of the Western economies.[55]

In light of the recent increase in Western capital investments in Eastern Europe, it is worthy to note that while East-West commodity trade is largely "monetary" and multilateral, East-West joint investment relations are largely expressed in "kind." In other words, Western investors typically take their interest, profits, and repayments in the commodities which result from the investment rather than in convertible currencies or gold. This actually works as a safeguard for the investor in view of possible instability of the CMEA country's price level and currency. One possible form of hedging in the case of monetary returns would be to include in contracts a provision which escalates the value of interest and repayments for price level increases in the nation whose currency is to serve as medium of exchange.[56]

Still, there are many other more immediate problems. Difficulties arise when technological and organizational adjustments are required of socialist partners, and these demands produce problems and tensions that hamper further cooperation. An extremely significant problem is that of transfer pricing, in which the socialist partners are usually exposed to two disadvantages. First, the prices of licenses, technology, and acquisition of equipment tends to be high. Secondly, the prices paid by the Western partner for intermediate products supplied by the socialist countries may be too low. Such low prices reflect not only the bargaining advantage of the Western partner, but also inaccurate accounting systems and exchange rates used in the socialist countries.[57]

Joint Ventures

In an ideological sense, forms of economic cooperation and joint ownership ventures stand at opposite extremes. In the former, management by the company is not a right vested in ownership, but a contractual commitment assumed for a specified period of time. It is the relative shift of the East Europeans from import to domestic production orientation which has fostered the emergence of the joint venture. Whereas the economic cooperation agreements largely substitute a management for an entrepreneurial role, joint venture agreements generally include the traditional capitalist incentive, which is rewards for the risks taken. Both forms, however, serve to increase the capability of Eastern enterprise, to utilize idle capacities, to develop resources, and to promote Eastern exports. In both forms also, payment may be made in cash, compensation, switch deals, or reciprocal deliveries, all of which will be discussed later. The basic difference between the two lies in the form of financing the transfer of capital, technology, and management. Whereas economic cooperation agreements are generally financed through loans and credits with a scheduled repayment of capital, payment of interest, and remuneration for technology in royalties and for management in fees, the joint ventures are generally financed by the investment of risk capital by both partners, with payment principally in the form of a share in the earnings.[58]

It is only in the last three years that the CMEA has officially opened up the possibility for joint ventures, in spite of individual state actions. At the CMEA meetings in October 1972 in Moscow and in June 1973 in Budapest, CMEA foreign trade specialists agreed for the first time that all forms of economic cooperation with capitalist countries are acceptable provided that they contribute to socialist economic development. Nevertheless, only three Eastern European socialist countries have so far issued special legal provisions facilitating the creation of joint ventures—Yugoslavia, Romania, and Hungary—while of the rest, only Poland is seriously considering such action. Surely it represents the most ambitious form of economic cooperation with the West so far. Whereas those joint ventures operating within the socialist country are intended to modernize domestic production or infrastructure and to generate hard-currency exports, those operating outside the socialist country are basically aimed at expanding the exports of industrial goods from the socialist country.[59] Although these joint venture agreements do not involve ownership of private property, the Western firms are entitled to many of the rights in the Western legal tradition; in addition to sharing in earnings, they participate in policy, planning, and management.[60]

Bulgaria considers joint ventures superfluous, since it feels it can obtain Western technology through various other forms of cooperation, financed through loans rather than by investment on a share basis. However, it is felt that the real reason is that of ideology, which is particularly strong. Czechoslovakia abstains also, and will probably continue to do so in the foreseeable future; it is felt by Western sources that Russian influence and fear of West German economic domination are the two major forces which have dampened interest there. Although joint ventures are under discussion in East Germany, it is felt that its relatively good position in regard to investment capital and the influence of the Soviets will delay immediate action.[61]

Of the countries under consideration, Romania by far has the most liberal outlook concerning joint ventures, which are to play a particularly significant role in future development. The law provides for foreign participation in joint ventures in the fields of industry, agriculture, construction, tourism, transport, and scientific and technical cooperation. Although there is a requirement for 51 percent Romanian ownership, that applies only to ventures inside Romania, and not to similar organizations set up in third countries.[62] The foreign partner may transfer 100 percent of his profits, and the rate of taxation on such profits is less than that of Yugoslavia, which initiated East-West joint ventures.[63]

In contrast to the Romanian attitude, Hungary has adopted joint ventures only as a last resort, and primarily for obtaining Western technology. Generally, such joint ventures may be formed only for trade and services; however, when economically justified, the joint ventures may take part directly in production. The focus of discussions in Hungary concerning joint ventures has been on the proprietary nature of capital participation, for even minority foreign ownership is difficult for the government to contemplate. However, it is extremely difficult in the case of Hungary to estimate exactly how much of the hesitance is due to political-ideological misgivings, how much to Soviet opposition to such ventures, and how much to purely economic factors. On the other hand, in contrast to the Yugoslav model, the Hungarian government guarantees full transferability of profits and repayment of capital indemnity for damages suffered by Western companies as a result of Hungarian government action, subordination of employee relationships to the government contract, and flexibility in allocating control for specific functions. Still, the potential for joint ventures is uncertain at the present time due to the government's attitude in general.[64]

The Poles have been considering the possibility of foreign joint ventures and regulations that would permit equity investment on the basis of Polish majority control, with provision for shared management responsibilities and for repatriation of profits. (We recall the story circulating recently about good and bad news: the good news was that Pan-Am was going to enter a joint venture with the Poles; the bad news was that Pan-Am would retain management control). Still, no new regulations have been published, although Polish officials maintain that Western firms should go ahead and make their proposals, which would be considered by the Poles. At any rate, such possibilities might well open up new arrangements.[65]

There are several problems inherent in joint venture arrangements with Eastern bloc countries. Marxist doctrine, fears of foreign economic domination, and the Soviet Union's strong stand against such arrangements cause Eastern European hesitancy. A major problem involves the percentage of shares, and the difficulty here is not primarily the distribution of profits, but control of management. Demarcation of markets is another problem to consider, and Western firms must attempt to escape the situation that Poland and the USSR find themselves in. They jointly manufacture trucks, and have ended up competing against one another for sales of their mutual product.[66]

One consideration increasingly taken into account in East-West joint ventures has been the longevity of the arrangement, important due to two major aspects: the degree to which socialist countries would be subject to Western economic fluctuations, and the possibility that the socialist partner will be able to continue production independently. Irregular withdrawals of invested capital on the part of the Western partner could upset bilateral balancing plans. Several methods have been discussed, including agreements that after a certain number of years the socialist partner could buy the shares held by the Western partner, and agreements allowing for the gradual phase-out of the Western partner. Such policies to limit the life of a specific joint venture in no way preclude the establishment of new agreements, and the continual creation of new joint ventures would allow for the incorporation of specific activities of joint ventures into general economic planning. However, since the concept of joint ventures is completely new to the socialist states, only experience will show which forms of compromise will be most effective.[67]

Switch Financing

Switch financing is primarily triangular payments through third country credits. In its present form, it usually involves the transfer of credits from within one bilateral trading agreement to provide convertible currency with which an Eastern European country may purchase Western exports. The clearing dollars that arise are the result of trading within a bilateral agreement, on which one partner has been unable to take up his full quota of goods. However, such clearing dollars cannot necessarily be used for all possible purchases from the country of origin. Since the clearing is actually in nonconvertible dollars, three things must be particularly taken into consideration: the stability of the country, the restrictiveness of the export quota list used in relation to clearing dollars, and the ease of using a certain country's bilateral agreements for switch dealing.[68]

In East-West trade, the use of clearing dollars has become more and more popular. Ironically, it is the developed countries who no longer have bilateral payments agreements among themselves, who directly benefit commercially from the switch transactions. At the same time, a switch transaction without their involvement would reduce the transaction to multilateral barter, probably of endless duration and complexity. Payments problems are lessened by switching, government authorities are helpful in their execution, and clearing currencies are now often negotiable against convertible currencies. Until East-West trade increases to a respectable level, and until Eastern goods are readily acceptable in Western markets, bottlenecks will continue to underscore the necessity and importance of switch transactions. In terms of global trade, the switch financing is insignificant, but it has been estimated that one-third of East-West trade at the present is due to switch transactions. Simply stated, where bilateralism exists, switch is the necessary evil it carries with it.[69]

One tactic often used by Eastern European buyers is to ask for bids on the basis of payment in convertible currencies, subject to approval by the Foreign Exchange authorities. Once the bid is in, it is discovered that the convertible currency payment cannot be made, and that clearing is necessitated, which involves clearing house discounts. Consequently, Western sellers have been advised to adjust their prices accordingly.[70] It has been contended that switching clearly favors debtors rather than creditors, the latter of whom are given the "unexciting choice" between purchasing goods they do not want and accumulating balances earning a rather low rate of interest.[71] However, other considerations should not be forgotten. For example, the American exporter might well welcome the arrangement, due to his distinct disadvantage in comparison to the West European exporter, since the latter has at his disposal export-minded state-owned credit insurance which allows the Eastern partner favorable payment conditions. Until the U.S. government becomes more competitive in that area, a switch proposal to the Eastern buyer might well counterbalance the attractiveness of West European payment terms.[72]

Barter

Barter agreements, under which a Western exporter to the East undertakes, as a condition of sale, to accept in payment certain products from the East which it will probably resell, are becoming less and less used. And they should be. They are unnecessarily burdensome to the Western supplier, and in the long run they work to the disadvantage of the Eastern country, since it implies the deferring of development of more effective marketing channels. In general, barter reflects Eastern difficulties in finding markets for their low-quality goods.[73]

There can be no doubt that barter arrangements are due to the shortage of convertible currencies in the East and to the lack of long-term credit terms available to them. There can also be no doubt that it is a great impediment to the expansion of East-West trade. Barter often results in unfavorable prices for the goods exported from the East and dissatisfaction from the importing nation which does not necessarily want that type of goods. In addition, the Western partner may be required to take in payment goods which have little or no relationship to the products with which he normally deals. Consequently, there has developed a new type of trading institution to dispose of such goods. A related problem is the re-exporting of such goods and the competition that it offers. In time, the Eastern countries will have to develop their own marketing expertise in connection with Western markets, instead of relying on Western firms to dispose of their goods.[74]

Other Forms of Arrangements

Compensation involves payment for an import into Eastern Europe with a predetermined quantity of a specific merchandise or commodity, unlike barter, which offers payment from a choice of a list of products, and usually expressed in dollars. Unlike clearing, compensation calls for the immediate balancing of transactions. Usually, compensation involves only a certain percentage of the transaction. Eastern European countries have generally aimed at 50 to 60 percent compensation, whereas Western firms have been fairly successful at lowering that percentage to 20 to 25 percent.[75]

Parallel trade is similar to barter, except that it involves two contracts, and the value of the goods exchanged need not match. It is preferable to compensation deals, since the Western firm at least has some choice in the product. In general, however, as with barter and compensation, it is often advisable for the Western firm to find an agent who specializes in disposing of such goods.[76]

Licensing is widely used in East-West trade, but it has not been emphasized here since the reader is well aware of its advantages and disadvantages. It should be noted, however, that the purchase of licenses aggravates the balance-of-payments problems of the CMEA countries vis-a-vis the West. Exports to the West under such agreements are not really advantageous for the Eastern countries, because of the competition of the firms which grant the licenses. The oligopolistic markets of Western countries are dominated by MNCs that put heavy emphasis on product diversification, trademarks, publicity and sales promotion, and only a very sharp price competition, when allowed by the agreement, would bring effective results.[77]

In general, the trends are favorable for the development of more sophisticated patterns of agreements between East and West partners. While barter, compensation, parallel trade, and switch financing will not die out overnight, competitive pressures and economic realities are forcing the Eastern countries more and more to shift to straight sales, to licensing, to loose forms of economic cooperation, and eventually to joint ventures. The urgent need for know-how, management, and marketing assistance has forced Eastern enterprises to seek more active participation with Western firms.[78] Until the archaic forms of trade are fully a thing of the past, however, such trade as exists between East and West will be artificially restricted.

NOTES

1. Carl H. McMillan, Changing Perspectives In East-West Commerce (Lexington: Heath, 1974), pp. 140, 144.
2. Ibid., p. 140.
3. Committee for Economic Development, East-West Trade: A Common Policy For the West (New York: Committee for Economic Development, 1965), pp. 27-28.
4. Harold B. Scott, "The Outlook for U.S.-East European Trade," East Europe 19 (November 1970): 10.
5. Robert W. Dean, West German Trade With the East: The Political Dimension (New York: Praeger, 1974), p. 16.
6. R. C. Fischer, "The European Community," in East-West Business Transactions, ed. Robert Starr (New York: Praeger, 1974), pp. 60-62.
7. Committee for Economic Development, op. cit., pp. 28-29.
8. "Nations Should Give Less Credit Unto Nations," The Economist 254 (March 15, 1975): 104.
9. E. G. Kamenov, "Some Problems In Economic Relations Between Socialist and Capitalist Countries," in Economic Development For Eastern Europe, ed. M. C. Kaser (New York: Martin's, 1968), p. 171.
10. Organization for Economic Cooperation and Development, Trade Measures and Adjustment of the Balance of Payments (Paris: OECD, 1971), pp. 57-59.
11. Dean, op. cit., pp. 18-19, 46, 67-70.
12. Axel Lebahn, "The Federal Republic of Germany," in East-West Business Transactions, ed. Robert Starr (New York: Praeger, 1974), pp. 79-85.

13. "Bonn zahlt Milliarden in die DDR-Kasse," *Frankfurter Allgemeine Zeitung*, May 22, 1975, p. 4.

14. "Der Kredit fuer Polen kostet Bonn mehr als eine Milliarde Mark an Zinsen," *Frankfurter Allgemeine Zeitung*, August 5, 1975, p. 1.

15. "Die deutsch-polnische Vereinbarung stoesst auch jenseits der Oder auf Kritik und Ablehnung," *Frankfurter Allgemeine Zeitung*, August 5, 1975, p. 2.

16. "Schmidts finanzielle Zusagen an Polen stossen bei der Opposition auf Widerspruch," *Frankfurter Allgemeine Zeitung*, August 4, 1975, p. 1.

17. "It's the fine print that counts," *The Economist* 256 (August 9, 1975): 37-38.

18. Dean, op. cit., pp. 31, 190, 216.

19. Julian D. M. Lew, "The United Kingdom," in *East-West Business Transactions*, ed. Robert Starr (New York: Praeger, 1974), pp. 101-04.

20. Nikolai V. Nikitkin, "Financing East-West Transactions—Use of United Kingdom-Based Institutions," in *Financing East-West Business Transactions*, ed. American Management Association (New York: American Management Association, 1968), p. 16.

21. "U.K. Loan to Comecon," *East Europe* 21 (May 1972): 31.

22. "Paper Crack," *The Economist* 255 (May 31, 1975): 75-76.

23. Thomas A. Wolf, "East-West Trade Credit Policy: A Comparative Analysis," in *U.S. Financing of East-West Trade*, ed. Paul Marer (Bloomington: International Development Research Center, 1975), p. 151.

24. Ibid., p. 182.

25. James C. Cruse and David G. Wigg, "The Role of Eximbank in U.S. Exports and East-West Trade," in *U.S. Financing of East-West Trade*, ed. Paul Marer (Bloomington: International Development Research Center, 1975), p. 67.

26. Ibid., p. 70.

27. "U.S. Industry, Government Officials, Soviet Spokesman Call For Trade Continuity," *Commerce Today* 5 (March 3, 1975): 20.

28. "Trade With Socialist Nations Maintains Favorable Balance," *Commerce Today* 5 (August 4, 1975): 23.

29. William A. Dymsza, "East-West Trade: Types of Business Arrangements," in *China, the U.S.S.R. and Eastern Europe: A U.S. Trade Perspective*, ed. John K. Ryans, Jr., Anant R. Negandhi, and James C. Baker (Kent: Kent State University, 1974), p. 115.

30. McMillan, op. cit., p. 140.

31. Franklyn D. Holzman, *Foreign Trade Under Central Planning* (Cambridge: Harvard University, 1974), p. 205.

32. United States Department of Commerce, "Trading and Investing in Romania," Overseas Business Reports OBR 73-36 (August 1973): 18.

33. Thomas W. Hoya, "Regulation of East-West Business Transactions by Market-Economy Countries: The United States," in East-West Business Transactions, ed. Robert Starr (New York: Praeger, 1974), pp. 10-11.

34. Thomas A. Wolf, U.S. East-West Trade Policy (Lexington: Heath, 1973), p. 71.

35. Miles J. Lambert, "CCC Financing of Agricultural Sales to the USSR and Eastern Europe," in U.S. Financing of East-West Trade, ed. Paul Marer (Bloomington: International Development Research Center, 1975), pp. 203-12.

36. Paul Marer, "Perspective on the Issues and the Debate," in U.S. Financing of East-West Trade, ed. Paul Marer (Bloomington: International Development Research Center, 1975), pp. 11-12.

37. Cruse and Wigg, op. cit., p. 74.

38. Douglas R. Bohi, "An Evaluation of the Role of Eximbank and Its Promotion of East-West Trade," in U.S. Financing of East-West Trade, ed. Paul Marer (Bloomington: International Development Research Center, 1975), pp. 79, 90-91.

39. Wolf, U.S. East-West Trade Policy, op. cit., pp. 92-93.

40. Walter C. Sauer, "Eximbank Credits Back East-West Trade," Columbia Journal of World Business 8 (Winter 1973): 57.

41. United States Department of Commerce, "World Trade Outlook for Eastern Europe, Union of Soviet Socialist Republics and People's Republic of China," Overseas Business Reports OBR 75-19 (March 1975): 2.

42. Stanley J. Marcuss, "New Light on the Export-Import Bank," in U.S. Financing of East-West Trade, ed. Paul Marer (Bloomington: International Development Research Center, 1975), p. 258.

43. Ibid., pp. 266-67.

44. "Eximbank May Face Lending Constraints For the First Time," Commerce Today 4 (June 24, 1974): 29.

45. John P. Hardt and George D. Holliday, "East-West Financing by Eximbank and National Interest Criteria," in U.S. Financing of East-West Trade, ed. Paul Marer (Bloomington: International Development Research Center, 1975), p. 296.

46. Leon Zurawicki, "The Cooperation of the Socialist State With the MNCs," Columbia Journal of World Business 10 (Spring 1975): 109.

47. "Bulgaria, Meeting Most Goals, Sets More Ambitious Objectives," Commerce Today 4 (August 19, 1974): 28.

48. "New Bulgarian Decrees Encourage Cooperation With Foreign Firms," Commerce Today 5 (December 9, 1974): 30.

49. United States Department of Commerce, "Doing Business With Czechoslovakia," Overseas Business Reports OBR 74-15 (June 1974): 20.

50. "Barriers Go Down," The Economist 255 (April 26, 1975): 111-12.

51. United States Department of Commerce, "Trading In Poland," Overseas Business Reports OBR 73-50 (October 1973): 4.

52. United States Department of Commerce, "Trading In Hungary," Overseas Business Reports OBR 74-32 (July 1974): 28.

53. United States Department of Commerce, "Romania," Foreign Economic Trends ET 74-093 (September 1974): 4.

54. United States Department of Commerce, OBR 73-36, op. cit., p. 1.

55. Zurawicki, op. cit., p. 112.

56. Holzman, op. cit., pp. 223-24.

57. Zurawicki, op. cit., p. 112.

58. John B. Holt, "New Roles for Western Multinationals in Eastern Europe," Columbia Journal of World Business 8 (Fall 1973): 131-32.

59. McMillan, op. cit., p. 24.

60. Holt, op. cit., p. 132.

61. Ibid., pp. 136-37.

62. Zygmunt Nagorski, Jr., The Psychology of East-West Trade (New York: Mason and Lipscomb, 1974), p. 116.

63. Holt, op. cit., p. 135.

64. Ibid., pp. 135-36.

65. United States Department of Commerce, "Poland," Foreign Economic Trends ET 74-017 (April 1974): 7.

66. "East Bloc: Where the Demand for Trucks is Blooming," Business Week 2403 (October 20, 1975): 60.

67. Zurawicki, op. cit., pp. 113-14.

68. A. Maxwell Stamp, "Services By Specialist Organizations Which Encourage East-West Transactions," in Financing East-West Business Transactions, ed. American Management Association, Inc. (New York: American Management Association, 1968), pp. 47-48.

69. Charles H. Baudoin, "The Use of Switch Financing to Facilitate East-West Business Transactions," in Financing East-West Business Transactions, ed. American Management Association, Inc. (New York: American Management Association, 1968), pp. 28-29, 32.

70. John P. Morgan, "The Financial Aspects of East-West Trade," Columbia Journal of World Business 8 (Winter 1973): 55.

71. Stanislaw Wasowski, "East-West Trade and the Pattern of World Trade," in East-West Trade and the Technology Gap: A Political and Economic Appraisal, ed. Wasowski (New York: Praeger, 1970), p. 176.

72. Baudoin, op. cit., p. 30.

73. Committee for Economic Development, op. cit., p. 24.

74. James R. Basche, Jr., East-West Trade: The Lessons From Experience (New York: Conference Board, 1971), pp. 24-25.

75. Dymsza, op. cit., p. 124.

76. Stamp, op. cit., p. 47.

77. Zurawicki, op. cit., p. 111.

78. Holt, op. cit., p. 138.

CHAPTER

8

PROBLEMS ARISING IN EAST-WEST TRADE

It is quite obvious by now that major obstacles lie in the path of East-West trade. We have touched upon some of the major difficulties, which include foremost bilateralism and inconvertibility. Also mentioned were the general differences between the economic systems, different legal frameworks affecting trade, financing difficulties, political influences, and restrictions on the types of business arrangements which can be implemented. This chapter deals with significant problems, but problems which are of a more temporary nature than those already mentioned.

WESTERN DISCRIMINATORY PRACTICES

The European Common Market is the single largest importing and exporting market for the CMEA countries outside their own bloc. Consequently, it is against the European Economic Community (EEC) that the loudest complaints are issued due to high customs duties, quantitative restrictions, nontariff and paratariff restrictions. It must be noted, however, that the EEC does not discriminate against the CMEA per se. Still, the restrictions present special difficulties for the CMEA members due to their different economic systems; that is, unlike capitalist countries, the Comecon members find it difficult to overcome the obstacles created by the EEC. Of special importance are the agricultural policies of the EEC, which affect the CMEA countries most. In addition to these general restrictions, the EEC countries apply some policy tools only to CMEA members, such as quantitative restrictions and the systems of licensing imports.[1] On the other hand, the tariff policies of the EEC have been said to have little effect regarding East-West trade, owing to the particular pricing system the Comecon members employ.[2]

Generally, in East-West trade there have been two major deterrents to increased trade besides those mentioned specifically: exports from East to West have involved the difficulty of reducing trade policies and practices to a common denominator both market-directed and centrally planned economies. In the other direction, trade has been hampered by the West's denial of certain exports which might directly or indirectly strengthen the military potential of a communist country. The first obstacle has caused adjustment in General Agreement on Tariffs and Trade (GATT) principles. This will be discussed but we now wish to describe discriminatory practices of the United States which hinder the expansion of East-West trade.

We have already referred to credit policy restrictions of the United States in connection with Comecon nations, and to the Johnson Default Act, in particular. Both the Export Control Act and the Battle Act adversely affected such trade. The first act made illegal the export of goods deemed to be important to our national security, and was most strictly applied to trade with the Eastern bloc. The Battle Act, passed under the influence of the Korean War, was an attempt by the United States to enlist the cooperation of other Western nations in doing the same thing.[3] More recently, the Trade Act of 1974 is also quite politically motivated, and represents an attempt on our part to regulate domestic policies of the East bloc countries.

The most effective obstacle, however, has been the denial of MFN treatment to members of Comecon. The basic attitude toward foreign trade among the Western nations is embodied in GATT, which assumes that no direct government controls are to be exercised over trade in "normal times." Second, tariffs on imports are to be applied without discrimination by place of origin. However, in the socialist countries, quantitative control of international trade has been the rule rather than the exception, and is an essential part of the overall national plan. There, tariffs have virtually no function. Since the Western governments cannot meaningfully compare the principles and practices followed, they have been hesitant to extend MFN status to the members of CMEA, and have been unwilling to apply GATT standards in dealing with them.[4]

One difficulty involved in the tariff situation is that CMEA markets are much less price sensitive than those of the market economies. In fact, regardless of the level of tariff in a centrally planned economy, imported commodities are ordinarily sold at the same price as comparable domestically produced goods, for the differences between the prices of imported and internally produced goods are equalized by offsetting taxes or subsidies. In addition, import decisions of the CMEA countries are not primarily based on price.[5] We have mentioned already the entry of several CMEA members into GATT, and the conditions under which they were admitted. There is obviously no easy solution to the problem, which in the long run must depend on the future development of "market socialism." But given the differences in economic systems, we cannot expect the CMEA countries to multilateralize all their trade, to give up their mutual trade agreements, or to completely revamp their infrastructures and pricing systems.[6]

While the MFN deterrent is very real, it is also largely psychological. Many East Europeans feel that the lack of MFN treatment for them is a form of punishment, or at the very least an unwelcome mat. Granted that the absence of MFN removes all possibilities for trade of certain products, for others it simply destroys the initiative to aggressively promote sales. Even should MFN treatment be given to each of the Comecon nations, it is anticipated that its effect on trade would not be overwhelming.[7] The many other obstacles which we have discussed are sufficient deterrents in themselves.

THE QUESTION OF DUMPING

Generally, dumping is defined as selling abroad at a lower price than at home. Because of the irrational pricing systems used by the Comecon countries, however, it is very hard to determine whether or not actual dumping has occurred. For one thing, comparison of domestic and export prices is a misleading criterion of dumping in such a case since the currencies of the centrally planned economies are grossly overvalued. Secondly, relative domestic prices in the CMEA states reflect subsidies and sales taxes introduced to satisfy domestic, fiscal, and other requirements. Thirdly, the East bloc countries have a different concept of "cost of production" from that of the West. Finally, as we have initially stressed, export and import decisions are not independent of each other, as they generally are in the market economies.[8]

In addition, planning difficulties among the centrally planned states cause dumping problems. Due to shortages in hard-currency reserves, sudden deficits require appropriate action by the state, which usually is found in the exporting of items in temporary surplus supply or that are allocated to low-priority use at home. Because the exporting is so urgent, it becomes profitable even at prices that involve a nominal loss. Accordingly, Western markets may suffer disruption. The only real guide that the Western importer has to go on is the market price of either domestic or other foreign suppliers. Even such a guide, however, is not sufficient evidence of dumping per se. The real problem is to determine whether or not products being sold by the CMEA countries at below market prices are a normal export or a crisis. If it is the latter case, the goods could be subjected to a countervailing tariff under our antidumping laws.[9]

It is generally agreed that each Western country has the freedom to restrict imports from the East that would cause market disruption. The problems have not been too great in the past for several reasons. First, the volume of East-West trade is negligible as far as the Western partners are concerned. The second reason is the desire on the part of the Eastern states to expand East-West trade; they fear that outright dumping would provoke hostile action on the part of the Western partner. Third, the East Europeans have a general reputation for good commercial conduct.[10] Nevertheless, in a trading relationship where one partner's costs are unknown and sometimes even undeterminable, and its prices are arbitrarily set through a political rather than economic process, the dangers of dumping are greatly increased. In order to safeguard the interests of their own industries, the countries in the West have often been obliged to restrict imports of certain goods from the East.[11]

OTHER PROBLEMS

There are numerous other lesser problems affecting East-West trade. Difficulties of a legal nature, for instance, complicate such trade. Since on the Eastern side the state is the actual commercial unit in foreign trade transactions, it is the ultimate legal arbiter of any conflicts that might arise. In other words, there is no neutral legal authority to which an injured party can appeal. The absence of laws which would protect Western property is another factor which gives rise to a feeling of legal insecurity in the West. However, the bloc states are members of the Union Convention of Paris for the protection of industrial property, and that has lessened Western fears to some extent.[12]

Some contend that the presence of socialist countries as buyers and sellers facing individual Western firms places the firms at a distinct disadvantage. Others contend it works to the advantage of the Western partner, because the Eastern unit operates according to plan and offers more certainty than would an individual firm. However, those accustomed to see in competition the sole guarantee against arbitrary price rises, and so on, approach the transaction with some amount of fear. Unlike Western monopolies, however, socialist foreign-trade enterprises are alien to any spirit of profiteering and to the desire to exploit the needs and difficulties of their trading partners.[13] Besides, private, profit-seeking firms will not grant terms which are below their own minimum costs plus a profit which they consider adequate. In addition, the Eastern buyers and sellers are not judged on their ability to make profits, as are the Western partners. Financing terms often play a much larger role in their considerations than do final prices.[14]

There are less specific problems. The very unfamiliarity of Western enterprises in doing business with socialist countries handicaps the expansion of East-West trade. Furthermore, Westerners, particularly Americans, have strong emotional feelings about dealing with communist countries.[15] In regard to both of these factors, the most inhibiting influence now seems to be the continuing restriction on the freedom of Western firms to find out for themselves, through direct contacts, where the most fruitful and productive ventures might be. Eastern Europeans are still quite suspicious that foreigners will exploit such commercial contacts to the detriment of Eastern economic and even military interests.[16] The process of improving relations is no easy task. The past decades have resulted in a legacy of distrust and suspicion that will not disappear overnight. Also, current problems indicate that the development of East-West trade is not immune to set-backs, which the wisdom of hindsight relating to recent wheat deals well illustrates.[17]

The United States is at a disadvantage compared to other Western countries due to our general foreign policy and our economic policies, including the withholding of MFN treatment and our noncompetitive credit policies. On the other hand, there is one unique advantage which we do indeed have—the joint venture concept is, as indicated, becoming more and more a reality in East-West trade: to the extent that it does become a major force, the ingenuity of the American businessman provides the United States with a flexibility and a competence based on worldwide experience superior to both our West European and Japanese competitors.[18] Moreover, there are signs that the United States has come to realize that our former aggressive policy of economic warfare designed to contain the communist countries is completely ineffective and inappropriate given the recent emphasis on detente, the lack of cohesion of the Western countries in regard to such a policy, and the relative economic strength of the CMEA countries.[19]

We have seen that the role of foreign trade in the CMEA countries is different from that of the West, and that the patterns of foreign trade, the balance-of-payments problems, and the commodity structure of exports and imports all restrict East-West trade to a great extent. We have seen, too, that the fundamental dilemma of CMEA integration is still unresolved; somehow, the Eastern countries must strike a balance between national and supranational interests. It is not likely that the CMEA states will abandon their preference for planned economy. On the other hand, there is a significant move toward planned market economy. In fact, the direction taken by the economic reforms is probably the most decisive factor in determining whether or not, in the long run, multilateralism and convertibility are feasible. In spite of transitional problems, frictions, and incongruities, the reforms thus hold the key to the future development of East-West trade in general and to rational economic integration in particular. After all, there is a lesson to be learned from the creation and development of the EEC, whose members cast aside differences that were seemingly overwhelming in recognition of the fact that all could gain from economic cooperation.

NOTES

1. Pawel Bozyk, Poland As A Trading Partner (Warsaw: Interpress, 1972), pp. 126-29.
2. John P. DeGara, Trade Relations Between the Common Market and the Eastern Bloc (Bruges: Tempelhof, 1964), p. 58.
3. Franklyn D. Holzman, Foreign Trade Under Central Planning (Cambridge: Harvard University, 1974), pp. 193-94.
4. Nicolas Spulber, Socialist Management and Planning: Topics in Comparative Socialist Economics (Bloomington: Indiana University, 1971), pp. 137-38.
5. Holzman, op. cit., pp. 152-53.
6. Ibid., pp. 212-13.
7. Harold B. Scott, "The Outlook for U.S.-East European Trade," East Europe 19 (November 1970): 10.
8. Holzman, op. cit., pp. 154-55.
9. Ibid., pp. 214-15.
10. Robert W. Dean, West German Trade With the East: The Political Dimension (New York: Praeger, 1974), pp. 11-12.
11. James R. Basche, Jr., East-West Trade: The Lessons From Experience (New York: Conference Board, 1971), p. 28.
12. Dean, op. cit., pp. 16-17.
13. E. G. Kamneov, "Some Problems In Economic Relations Between Socialist and Capitalist Countries," in Economic Development For Eastern Europe, ed. M. C. Kaser (New York: St. Martin's, 1968), p. 170.

14. Gunter Dufey, "Financing East-West Business," Columbia Journal of World Business 9 (Spring 1974): 40.

15. William A. Dymsza, "East-West Trade: Types of Business Arrangements," MSU Business Topics 19 (Winter 1971): 22.

16. Robert V. Roosa, "Building Bridges From Both Shores," in Financing East-West Business Transactions, ed. American Management Association (New York: American Management Association, 1968), p. 4.

17. United States Department of Commerce, "World Trade Outlook for Eastern Europe, Union of Soviet Socialist Republics and People's Republic of China," Overseas Business Reports OBR 74-13 (May 1974): 2.

18. Scott, op. cit., p. 12.

19. Thomas A. Wolf, U.S. East-West Trade Policy (Lexington: Heath, 1973), pp. 112, 116, 144.

APPENDIX
TRADE VALUE TABLES

Reprinted from William R. Kintner and Wolfgang Klaiber, Eastern Europe and European Security (New York: Dunellen, 1971), pp. 230-31, 242-43, 328-35, and 342-45.

TABLE A.1

Trade Value of the East European States with the USSR as a Percentage of Their Respective Total Trade Values, 1956-67

Year	Bulgaria	Czechoslovakia	East Germany	Hungary	Poland	Romania
1956	45.4	31.8	41.1	23.7	30.6	n.a.
1957	53.5	34.0	45.1	29.3	30.6	n.a.
1958	53.3	33.1	43.1	26.9	26.2	51.5
1959	52.2	35.6	45.2	29.7	29.8	47.4
1960	53.1	34.4	43.0	30.2	30.3	40.1
1961	52.1	33.6	43.8	33.5	30.6	40.4
1962	53.3	37.8	48.9	36.0	32.5	40.6
1963	53.5	38.9	48.6	34.3	33.7	41.9
1964	53.0	37.5	46.6	34.7	32.7	42.2
1965	51.1	36.9	42.8	35.6	33.1	38.8
1966	49.2	33.5	41.4	33.1	32.2	33.5
1967	51.3	35.1	42.0	34.7	35.3	28.2
Mean	51.7	35.2	44.3	31.8	31.5	40.4
Rank	6	3	5	2	1	4

n.a. = data not available.

TABLE A.2

Total East European Trade Value with the USSR as a Percentage of East European Net Material Product, 1956-67

Year	Bulgaria	Czechoslovakia	East Germany	Hungary	Poland	Romania
1956	6.0	4.4	4.7	3.2	1.0	n.a.
1957	8.0	4.8	6.0	3.8	0.9	n.a.
1958	7.8	4.6	5.4	3.8	0.7	3.6
1959	8.9	5.6	6.1	4.3	0.9	3.2
1960	9.8	5.7	5.9	4.6	0.9	3.3
1961	n.a.	5.7	6.0	5.5	0.9	3.6
1962	18.8*	6.6	6.9	6.1	1.1	3.8
1963	19.5	7.5	7.0	6.2	1.1	3.9
1964	20.4	7.9	7.2	6.7	1.1	3.9
1965	21.2	8.2	6.7	7.6	1.1	3.3
1966	22.0	6.8	6.8	6.6	1.1	2.9
1967	23.2	6.0	6.8	6.9	1.2	2.8
Mean	15.1	6.1	6.3	5.4	1.0	3.4
Rank	6	4	5	3	1	2

*The marked increase relative to the preceding figures is a result of a currency reevaluation.

n.a. = data not available.

TABLE A.3

Trade Value of the East European States with East Europe (Excluding the USSR) as a Percentage of Their Total Respective Trade Values, 1956-67

Year	Bulgaria	Czechoslovakia	East Germany	Hungary	Poland	Romania
1956	37.3	27.9	24.9	32.1	26.7	n.a.
1957	29.1	27.1	22.1	35.7	25.9	n.a.
1958	29.7	29.4	23.6	37.2	26.9	21.3
1959	28.0	29.2	24.7	35.3	28.1	25.8
1960	28.7	30.7	26.4	35.6	28.1	27.6
1961	30.0	32.1	28.6	34.7	28.5	25.0
1962	26.4	33.0	27.4	34.0	29.4	25.2
1963	26.9	31.8	27.5	32.8	28.9	23.3
1964	22.6	33.1	27.9	32.6	29.0	23.6
1965	23.7	33.6	28.8	31.2	29.8	23.2
1966	21.1	33.5	29.0	31.7	28.6	22.5
1967	22.7	34.3	29.2	31.5	27.6	20.6
Mean	27.2	31.3	26.7	33.7	28.1	23.8
Rank	3	5	2	6	4	1

n.a. = data not available.

TABLE A.4

Total East European Trade Value with East Europe (Excluding the USSR) as a Percentage of East European Net Material Product, 1956-67

Year	Bulgaria	Czechoslovakia	East Germany	Hungary	Poland	Romania
1956	4.9	3.9	2.9	4.4	0.9	n.a.
1957	4.3	3.8	3.0	4.6	0.8	n.a.
1958	4.4	4.1	3.0	5.2	0.8	1.5
1959	4.8	4.6	3.3	5.1	0.8	1.7
1960	5.3	5.1	3.6	5.4	0.8	2.3
1961	n.a.	5.5	3.9	5.7	0.9	2.2
1962	9.3*	5.8	3.9	5.8	1.0	2.3
1963	9.8	6.1	4.0	5.9	0.9	2.1
1964	8.7	7.0	4.3	6.3	1.0	2.2
1965	9.8	7.4	4.5	6.6	1.0	2.0
1966	9.4	6.8	4.7	6.3	1.0	1.9
1967	10.2	5.8	4.7	6.3	0.9	2.0
Mean	7.4	5.5	3.8	5.6	0.9	2.0
Rank	6	4	3	5	1	2

*The marked increase relevant to the preceding years is a result of a currency reevaluation.
n.a. = data not available.

TABLE A.5

Trade Value of the East European States with the Western World as a Percentage of Their Respective Total Trade Values, 1956-67

Year	Bulgaria	Czechoslovakia	East Germany	Hungary	Poland	Romania
1956	11.4	17.0	20.5	28.8	30.7	n.a.
1957	11.6	18.4	19.2	23.0	32.2	n.a.
1958	16.5	16.6	18.8	21.2	32.7	17.0
1959	18.2	15.7	17.9	22.4	29.4	15.3
1960	18.1	16.0	18.0	22.8	28.7	21.9
1961	11.1	17.7	17.8	21.6	29.2	25.3
1962	12.4	14.1	15.6	21.1	27.1	24.8
1963	13.2	15.0	15.7	23.3	26.1	24.1
1964	16.4	15.5	17.9	23.8	26.9	24.4
1965	16.9	16.4	19.3	23.5	25.0	26.7
1966	20.9	18.7	19.8	24.8	27.8	31.7
1967	17.5	17.4	18.5	24.1	26.7	37.1
Mean	15.4	16.5	18.3	23.4	28.5	24.8
Rank	1	2	3	4	6	5

n.a. = data not available.

TABLE A.6

East European Trade Value with the Western World as a Percentage of East European Net Material Product, 1956-67

Year	Bulgaria	Czechoslovakia	East Germany	Hungary	Poland	Romania
1956	1.1	2.6	2.4	3.9	1.0	n.a.
1957	1.7	2.6	2.6	2.9	1.0	n.a.
1958	2.4	2.3	2.2	3.0	0.9	1.2
1959	3.1	2.5	2.4	3.2	0.9	1.0
1960	3.3	2.7	2.5	3.5	0.9	1.8
1961	n.a.	3.0	2.4	3.5	0.9	2.2
1962	4.3	2.5	2.2	3.6	0.9	2.3
1963	4.8	2.9	2.3	4.2	0.9	2.2
1964	6.3	3.5	2.7	4.6	0.9	2.3
1965	7.0	3.7	3.0	5.0	0.9	2.3
1966	9.3	3.8	3.2	4.9	0.9	2.7
1967	7.8	3.0	3.0	4.8	0.9	3.6
Mean	4.6	2.9	2.6	3.9	0.9	2.2
Rank	6	4	3	5	1	2

n.a. = data not available.

TABLE A.7

East European Trade Dependence on the USSR: Mean Values and Rankings of Four Indicators, 1956-67

	Bulgaria	Czechoslovakia	East Germany	Hungary	Poland	Romania
1. Mean Trade Value with the USSR as a percent of Total Trade Value	51.7	35.2	44.3	31.8	31.5	40.4
Ranking	6	3	5	2	1	4
2. Mean Trade Value with the USSR as a percent of Net Material Product	15.1	6.1	6.3	5.4	1.0	3.4
Ranking	6	4	5	3	1	2
3. Mean Trade Value with East Europe as a percent of Total Trade Value	27.2	31.3	26.7	33.7	28.1	23.8
Ranking	3	5	2	6	4	1
4. Mean Trade Value with East Europe as a percent of Net Material Product	7.4	5.5	3.8	5.6	0.9	2.0
Ranking	6	4	3	5	1	2

TABLE A.8

East European Mean Trade Value with the USSR, with the Western World, and with the USSR and East Europe as a Percentage of Total Trade Value, 1956-67

	Bulgaria	Czechoslovakia	East Germany	Hungary	Poland	Romania
Mean East European Trade Value						
1. With the USSR as a percent of Total Trade Value	51.7	35.2	44.3	31.8	31.5	40.4
2. With the Western World as percent of Total Trade Value	15.4	16.5	18.3	23.4	28.5	24.8
3. With the USSR and East Europe as percent of Total Trade Value	78.9	66.5	71.0	65.5	59.6	64.2

BIBLIOGRAPHY

Amid-hozour, E., and J. Somogyi. "East-West Trade." Finance and Development 10 (June 1973): 32-37.

Aspaturian, Vernon V. "Marxism and the Meanings of Modernization." In The Politics of Modernization in Eastern Europe: Testing the Soviet Model, edited by Charles Gati, pp. 3-21. New York: Praeger, 1974.

Ausch, Sandor. "Problems of Bilateralism and Multilateralism in the External Trade and Payments System of the CMEA Countries." In Foreign Trade In A Planned Economy, edited by Imre Vajda and Mihaly Simai, pp. 61-100. Cambridge: Cambridge University Press, 1971.

_____. Theory and Practice of CMEA Cooperation. Budapest: Akademiai Kiado, 1972.

Babitchev, Eugene. "The International Bank for Economic Cooperation." In Money and Plan: Financial Aspects of East European Economic Reforms, edited by Gregory Grossman, pp. 129-52. Los Angeles: University of California Press, 1968.

Baker, James C. "United States Business Opportunities in East Europe." In China, the U.S.S.R. and Eastern Europe: A U.S. Trade Perspective, edited by John K. Ryans, Jr., Anant R. Negandhi, and James C. Baker, pp. 99-109. Kent, Ohio: Kent State University Press, 1974.

"Barriers Go Down." The Economist, April 26, 1975, pp. 111-12.

Basche, James R., Jr. East-West Trade: The Lessons From Experience. New York: Conference Board, 1971.

Baudoin, Charles H. "The Use of Switch Financing to Facilitate East-West Business Transactions." In Financing East-West Business Transactions, edited by American Management Association, Inc., pp. 28-32. New York: American Management Association, 1968.

Bergsten, C. Fred, ed. The Future of the International Economic Order: An Agenda For Research. Lexington, Massachusetts: Heath, 1973.

Black, Cyril E. "Eastern Europe in the Context of Comparative Modernization." In The Politics of Modernization in Eastern Europe: Testing the Soviet Model, edited by Charles Gati, pp. 22-39. New York: Praeger, 1974.

Bogomolov, O. "The International Market of the CMEA Countries." In The Market of Socialist Economic Integration, edited by T. Kiss, pp. 31-36. Budapest: Akademiai Kiado, 1973.

Bohi, Douglas R. "An Evaluation of the Role of Eximbank and Its Promotion of East-West Trade." In U.S. Financing of East-West Trade, edited by Paul Marer, pp. 75-93. Bloomington: International Development Research Center, 1975.

"Bonn zahlt Milliarden in die DDR-Kasse." Frankfurter Allgemeine Zeitung, May 22, 1975, p. 4.

Bozyk, Pawel. Poland As A Trading Partner. Warsaw: Interpress, 1972.

Brabant, Jozef M. P. van. Bilateralism and Structural Bilateralism in Intra-CMEA Trade. Rotterdam: Rotterdam University Press, 1973.

____. Essays on Planning in Eastern Europe. Rotterdam: Rotterdam University Press, 1974.

Brestel, Heinz. "Wenn drueben einer Westgeld hat." Frankfurter Allgemeine Zeitung, June 14, 1975, p. 11.

Brown, Alan A. "Towards A Theory of Centrally Planned Foreign Trade." In International Trade and Central Planning, edited by Alan A. Brown and Egon Neuberger, pp. 58-103. Los Angeles: University of California Press, 1968.

"Bulgaria, Meeting Most Goals, Sets More Ambitious Objectives." Commerce Today, August 19, 1974, p. 28.

Burks, R. V. "The Rumanian National Deviation: An Accounting." In Eastern Europe in Transition, edited by Kurt London, pp. 93-113. Baltimore: Johns Hopkins Press, 1966.

Burgess, Jay A. "The Socialist Republic of Romania." In East-West Business Transactions, edited by Robert Starr, pp. 272-310. New York: Praeger, 1974.

Campbell, Robert. "On the Theory of Economic Administration." In Industrialization In Two Systems, edited by Henry Rosovsky, pp. 186-203. New York: Wiley and Sons, 1966.

Caves, Richard E. and Ronald W. Jones. World Trade and Payments. Boston: Little, Brown and Co., 1973.

"Comecon Integration Program." East Europe 20 (August, 1971): 34-35.

"Comecon—The Next Five Years." Business International 22 (March 7, 1975): 76-78.

Committee for Economic Development. East-West Trade: A Common Policy For The West. New York: Committee for Economic Development, 1965.

"Communist Bloc Loans In Europe Seen Rising In 2nd Half From 1st." Wall Street Journal, October 16, 1975, p. 28.

"Comrades Unite." The Economist 256 (July 5, 1975): 123.

Cruse, James C., and David G. Wigg. "The Role of Eximbank in U.S. Exports and East-West Trade." In U.S. Financing of East-West Trade, edited by Paul Marer, pp. 49-74. Bloomington: International Development Research Center, 1975.

Csikos-Nagy, Bela. "Mutual Advantages In the Economic Cooperation." In The Market of Socialist Economic Integration, edited by T. Kiss, pp. 179-90. Budapest: Akademiai Kiado, 1973.

____. Socialist Economic Policy. New York: St. Martin's Press, 1973.

"Current Developments: Comecon Trade Plans." East Europe 21 (April 1972): 30.

"Current Developments: EEC Documents on Comecon." East Europe 23 (July 1974): 28.

"Current Developments: Romania." East Europe 21 (June 1972): 44-47.

"Current Developments: U.K. Loan to Comecon." East Europe 21 (May 1972): 31.

"Czechoslovakia Eyes Western Sources For Up-to-Date Technology, Equipment." Commerce Today 4 (April 15, 1974): 31.

"Czechoslovakia Faces Slower Growth: Trade Act Problems Delay U.S. Sales." Commerce Today 5 (April 18, 1975): 30-31.

Dean, Robert W. West German Trade With the East: The Political Dimension. New York: Praeger, 1974.

DeGara, John P. Trade Relations Between the Common Market and the Eastern Bloc. Bruges: Tempelhof, 1964.

Dellin, L. A. D. "Bulgaria: Tempest in a Teapot." In Reforms in the Soviet and Eastern European Economies, edited by L. A. D. Dellin and Hermann Gross, pp. 39-58. Lexington, Massachussetts: Lexington Books, 1972.

"Der Kredit fuer Polen kostet Bonn mehr als eine Milliarde Mark an Zinsen." Frankfurter Allgemeine Zeitung, July 29, 1975, p. 7.

"Der Ost-Export steigt kraeftig." Frankfurter Allgemeine Zeitung, July 29, 1975, p. 7.

"Die deutsch-polnische Vereinbarung stoesst auch jenseits der Oder auf Kritik und Ablehnung." Frankfurter Allgemeine Zeitung, August 5, 1975, p. 2.

Dobrin, Bogoslav. Bulgarian Economic Development Since World War II. New York: Praeger, 1973.

Dufey, Gunter. "Financing East-West Business." Columbia Journal of World Business 9 (Spring 1974): 37-41.

Dymsza, William A. "East-West Trade: Types of Business Arrangements." In China, the U.S.S.R. and Eastern Europe: A U.S. Trade Perspective, edited by John K. Ryans, Jr., Anant R. Negandhi and James C. Baker, pp. 118-31. Kent, Ohio: Kent State University Press, 1974.

____. "East-West Trade: Types of Business Arrangements." MSU Business Topics 19 (Winter, 1971): 22-28.

"East Bloc: Where the Demand for Trucks is Blooming." Business Week, October 20, 1975, p. 60.

"Eastern Europe: The East Bloc Looks Westward for Loans." Business Week, September 22, 1975, pp. 38-39.

"Economic Unit Formed By U.S., Hungarian Commerce Chambers." Commerce Today 5 (March 31, 1975): 23.

"EEC and Rumania: Wriggling Out." The Economist, July 19, 1975, pp. 28-29.

Evans, Douglas. The Politics of Trade: The Evolution of the Superbloc. New York: Wiley and Sons, 1974.

"Eximbank May Face Lending Constraints For the First Time." Commerce Today 4 (June 24, 1974): 29.

Fekete, Janos. "The Role of Monetary and Credit Policy in the Reform of Hungary's Economic Mechanism." In Money and Plan: Financial Aspects of East European Economic Reforms, edited by Gregory Grossman, pp. 57-59. Los Angeles: University of California Press, 1968.

Fischer, R. C. "The European Community." In East-West Business Transactions, edited by Robert Starr, pp. 51-78. New York: Praeger, 1974.

French, George T. "Problems in Conducting East-West Trade: One Company's Experience." In Financing East-West Business Transactions, edited by American Management Association, Inc., pp. 9-14. New York: American Management Association, 1968.

Gamarnikow, Michael. Economic Reforms in Eastern Europe. Detroit: Wayne State University Press, 1968.

____. "Introduction: Economics and Politics." In Reforms in the Soviet and Eastern European Economies, edited by L. A. D. Dellin and Hermann Gross, pp. 1-18. Lexington, Massachussetts: Lexington Books, 1972.

____. "Is Comecon Obsolete?," East Europe 17 (April, 1968): 12-18.

____. "Poland: On Again -- Off Again." In Reforms in the Soviet and Eastern European Economies, edited by L. A. D. Dellin and Hermann Gross, pp. 93-114. Lexington, Massachusetts: Lexington Books, 1972.

Garvy, George. "East European Credit and Finance in Transition." In Money and Plan: Financial Aspects of East European Economic Reforms, edited by Gregory Grossman, pp. 153-83. Los Angeles: University of California Press, 1968.

"German D. Rep.: Raw Materials Prices Dim Trade Prospects." Commerce Today 5 (August 4, 1975): 25.

Gilberg, Trond. Modernization in Romania Since World War II. New York: Praeger, 1975.

Grossman, Gregory. "Foreign Trade, Economic Reform, and Technology." In East-West Trade and the Technology Gap: A Political and Economic Appraisal, edited by Stanislaw Wasowski, pp. 151-54. New York: Praeger, 1970.

Grzbowski, Kazimierz. "Organization and Conduct of Foreign Trade in Countries With State-Planned Economies: Comecon." In East-West Business Transactions, edited by Robert Starr, pp. 117-36. New York: Praeger, 1974.

Haberler, Gottfried. "Theoretical Reflections on the Trade of Socialist Economies." In International Trade and Central Planning, edited by Alan A. Brown and Egon Neuberger, pp. 29-46. Los Angeles: University of California Press, 1968.

Hardt, John P., and George D. Holliday. "East-West Financing by Eximbank and National Interest Criteria." In U.S. Financing of East-West Trade, edited by Paul Marer, pp. 291-320. Bloomington: International Development Research Center, 1975.

Herman, Karl. "The Czechoslovak Socialist Republic." In East-West Business Transactions, edited by Robert Starr, pp. 169-86. New York: Praeger, 1974.

Hermann, Adolf. "Can Comecon Integrate?." East Europe 18 (May, 1969): 15-18.

____. "East-West Trade: What Happens in the '70s?." East Europe 19 (November 1970): 13-19.

Holt, John B. "New Roles for Western Multinationals in Eastern Europe." Columbia Journal of World Business 8 (Fall 1973): 131-39.

Holzman, Franklyn D. Foreign Trade Under Central Planning. Cambridge: Harvard University Press, 1974.

____. "Future East-West Economic Issues." In The Future of the International Economic Order: An Agenda for Research, edited by C. Fred Bergsten, pp. 265-92. Lexington, Massachusetts: Heath, 1973.

Hoya, Thomas W. "Regulation of East-West Business Transactions by Market-Economy Countries: The United States." In East-West Business Transactions, edited by Robert Starr, pp. 3-30. New York: Praeger, 1974.

"Hungary Aimes At Further Progress After Topping Planned Output Goals." Commerce Today 4 (September 2, 1974): 26.

"It's the Fine Print That Counts." The Economist, August 9, 1975, pp. 37-38.

Jamgotch, Nish, Jr. Soviet-East European Dialogue: International Regulations Of A New Type?." Stanford: Stanford University Press, 1968.

Kamenov, E. G. "Some Problems In Economic Relations Between Socialist and Capitalist Countries." In Economic Development For Eastern Europe, edited by M. C. Kaser, pp. 163-73. New York: St. Martin's Press, 1968.

Janssen, Richard F. "Balkans Forge Closer Economic Ties." Wall Street Journal, June 7, 1976, p. 4.

Kanet, Roger E. "Modernizing Interaction Within Eastern Europe." In The Politics of Modernization In Eastern Europe: Testing the Soviet Model, edited by Charles Gati, pp. 275-303. New York: Praeger, 1974.

Keohane, Robert O. and Joseph S. Nye. "World Politics and the International Economic System." In The Future of the International Economic Order: An Agenda for Research, edited by C. Fred Bergsten, pp. 115-79. Lexington, Massachusetts: Heath, 1973.

Kintner, William R., and Wolfgang Klaiber. Eastern Europe and European Security. New York: Dunellen, 1971.

Kiss, T. "The Development of the Forms of Economic Relations in the CMEA Integration." In The Market of Socialist Economic Integration, edited by T. Kiss, pp. 109-26. Budapest: Akademiai Kiado, 1973.

Klaiber, Wolfgang. "East-West Trade and U.S. Objectives in Eastern Europe." In East-West Trade and the Technology Gap: A Political and Economic Appraisal, edited by Stanislaw Wasowski, pp. 203-14. New York: Praeger, 1970.

Kormnov, Y. "International Industrial Specialization." In The Market of Socialist Economic Integration, edited by T. Kiss, pp. 143-48. Budapest: Akademiai Kiado, 1973.

Kover, K. "Internal Monetary Systems and Foreign Exchange Systems." In The Market of Socialist Economic Integration, edited by T. Kiss, pp. 213-19. Budapest: Akademiai Kiado, 1973.

Lambert, Miles J. "CCC Financing of Agricultural Sales to the USSR and Eastern Europe." In U.S. Financing of East-West Trade, edited by Paul Marer, pp. 203-12. Bloomington: International Development Research Center, 1975.

Laszlo, Andor. "Monetary Policy: A Help to Fostering International Cooperation." In Convertibility, Multilateralism and Freedom, edited by Wolfgang Schmitz, pp. 121-33. New York: Springer, 1972.

Lebahn, Axel. "The Federal Republic of Germany." In East-West Business Transactions, edited by Robert Starr, pp. 79-96. New York: Praeger, 1974.

Lew, Julian D. M. "The United Kingdom." In East-West Business Transactions, edited by Robert Starr, pp. 97-113. New York: Praeger, 1974.

Linder, Willy. "Hungary: Marching Forward." In Reforms in the Soviet and Eastern European Economies, edited by L. A. D. Dellin and Hermann Gross, pp. 79-92. Lexington, Massachussetts: Lexington Books, 1972.

Lyutov, A. "Economic Integration and the Socialist International Market." In The Market of Socialist Economic Integration, edited by T. Kiss, pp. 49-55. Budapest: Akademiai Kiado, 1973.

Machowski, Heinrich. "Toward A Socialist Economic Integration of Eastern Europe." In Eastern Europe in the 1970s, edited by Sylva Sinanian, Istvan Deak, and Peter C. Ludz, pp. 189-200. New York: Praeger, 1972.

"Mainland China Begins Common Market Ties." Wall Street Journal, September 16, 1975, p. 10.

Marcuss, Stanley J. "New Light on the Export-Import Bank." In U.S. Financing of East-West Trade, edited by Paul Marer, pp. 257-90. Bloomington: International Development Research Center, 1975.

Marer, Paul. "Perspective on the Issues and the Debate." In U.S. Financing of East-West Trade, edited by Paul Marer, pp. 3-44. Bloomington: International Development Research Center, 1975.

McMillan, Carl H. Changing Perspective in East-West Commerce. Lexington, Massachussetts: Heath, 1974.

Meerhaeghe, M. A. G. van. International Economic Institutions. New York: St. Martin's Press, 1971.

Meier, Viktor. "Schwierige Integration im Ostblock." Frankfurter Allgemeine Zeitung, July 16, 1975, p. 9.

Mikesell, Raymond F., and Jack N. Behrman. Financing Free World Trade With the Sino-Soviet Bloc. Princeton: Princeton University Press, 1958.

Montias, John Michael. Central Planning In Poland. Westport, Connecticut: Greenwood Press, 1962.

____. "Economic Nationalism in Eastern Europe: Forty Years of Continuity and Change." In Eastern Europe in Transition, edited by Kurt London, pp. 173-203. Baltimore: Johns Hopkins Press, 1966.

Morgan, John P. "The Financial Aspects of East-West Trade." Columbia Journal of World Business 8 (Winter 1973): 51-56.

Nagorski, Zygmunt, Jr. The Psychology of East-West Trade. New York: Mason and Lipscomb, 1974.

"Nations Should Give Less Credit Unto Nations." The Economist, March 15, 1975, p. 104.

"New Bulgarian Decrees Encourage Cooperation With Foreign Firms." Commerce Today 5 (December 9, 1974): 30.

Nikitkin, Nikolai V. "Financing East-West Transactions—Use of United Kingdom-Based Institutions." In Financing East-West Business Transactions, edited by American Management Association, pp. 14-18. New York: American Management Association, 1968.

Organization For Economic Cooperation and Development. Trade Measures and Adjustment of the Balance of Payments. Paris: OECD, 1971.

"Paper Crack." The Economist, May 31, 1975, pp. 75-76.

Pisar, Samuel. Coexistence and Commerce. New York: McGraw-Hill, 1970.

"Poland: Copper Major." The Economist, June 28, 1975, pp. 95-96.

"Poland: Industrial Expansion Spurs Machinery Need." Commerce Today 5 (August 4, 1975): 26.

"Polen und Frankreich demonstrienren 'privilegierte Beziehungen'." Frankfurter Allgemeine Zeitung, June 18, 1975, p. 4.

"Political Hurdles Stall Expansion Of EEC-Comecon Trade." Business International 23 (February 27, 1976): 71.

Ramsey, James A. "The 'Euroruble'—Competition or Convertibility?," Columbia Journal of World Business 3 (November-December 1968): 61-66.

Robinson, William F. The Pattern of Reform in Hungary: A Political, Economic and Cultural Analysis. New York: Praeger, 1973.

Rohleder, Claus D. "Rumania: The Laggard." In Reforms in the Soviet and Eastern European Economies, edited by L. A. D. Dellin and Hermann Gross, pp. 115-22. Lexington, Massachussetts: Lexington Books, 1972.

Roosa, Robert V. "Building Bridges From Both Shores." In Financing East-West Business Transactions, edited by American Management Association, pp. 4-9. New York: American Management Association, 1968.

"Rumania and the U.S.: Walnuts and After." The Economist, April 12, 1975, pp. 100-01.

Rurarz, Zdzislaw M. "Polish Experience and Practices In East-West Trade." In East-West Trade: An Analysis of Trade Between Western Nations and the Soviet Bloc, edited by American Management Association, pp. 46-51. New York: American Management Association, 1964.

Rusmich, Ladislav. "Financing The Investment Bank." (Interview) East Europe 20 (January 1971): 47-48.

Sauer, Walter C. "Eximbank Credits Back East-West Trade." Columbia Journal of World Business 8 (Winter 1973): 57-60.

Sawyer, Carole A. Communist Trade With Developing Countries: 1955-65. New York: Praeger, 1966.

Schaefer, Henry Wilcox. Comecon and the Politics of Integration. New York: Praeger, 1972.

"Schmidts finanzielle Zusagen an Polen stossen bei der Opposition auf Widerspruch." Frankfurter Allgemeine Zeitung, August 4, 1975, p. 1.

Schmitz, Wolfgang. "Convertibility, Multilateralism and Freedom: A Concept For Recovery and Prosperity." In Convertibility, Multilateralism and Freedom, edited by Wolfgang Schmitz, pp. vii-xii. New York: Springer, 1972.

____. "Monetary Dynamic Forces in East and West: Important Developments in the Seventies." In Convertibility, Multilateralism and Freedom, edited by Wolfgang Schmitz, pp. 219-40. New York: Springer, 1972.

Schultz, Lothar J. and Clifford A. Rathkopf, Jr. "The German Democratic Republic." In East-West Business Transactions, edited by Robert Starr, pp. 187-218. New York: Praeger, 1974.

Scott, Harold B. "The Outlook for U.S. - East European Trade." East Europe 19 (November 1970): 9-12.

Sellekaerts, Willy. "Economic Reforms in Eastern Europe." MSU Business Topics 18 (Autumn 1970): 20-26.

Selucky, Radoslav. Economic Reforms in Eastern Europe: Political Background and Economic Significance. New York: Praeger, 1972.

Shastitko, B. M. and Y. S. Shiryaev. "Interrelations With Non-Socialist Markets." In The Market of Socialist Economic Integration, edited by T. Kiss, pp. 159-65. Budapest: Akademiai Kiado, 1973.

Sik, Ota. "Czechoslovakia: Prohibitive Odds." In Reforms in the Soviet and Eastern European Economies, edited by L. A. D. Dellin and Hermann Gross, pp. 59-78. Lexington, Massachusetts: Lexington Books, 1972.

Simai, Mihaly. "Exports and Export Performance." In Foreign Trade In a Planned Economy, edited by Imre Vajda and Mihaly Simai, pp. 113-31. Cambridge: Cambridge University Press, 1971.

Sirc, Ljubo. Economic Devolution in Eastern Europe. New York: Praeger, 1969.

Smith, Glen Alden. Soviet Foreign Trade: Organization, Operations, and Policy, 1918-1971. New York: Praeger, 1973.

Soldaczuk, J. "Trade and Cooperation Among CMEA Member Countries." In The Market of Socialist Economic Integration, edited by T. Kiss, pp. 137-48. Budapest: Akademiai Kiado, 1973.

Spigler, Iancu. Economic Reform in Rumanian Industry. London: Oxford University Press, 1973.

Spulber, Nicolas. Socialist Management and Planning: Topics in Comparative Socialist Economics. Bloomington: Indiana University Press, 1971.

Staar, Richard F. The Communist Regimes in Eastern Europe. Stanford: Stanford University Press, 1971.

Stamp, A. Maxwell. "Services By Specialist Organizations Which Encourage East-West Transactions." In Financing East-West Business Transactions, edited by American Management Association, pp. 44-48. New York: American Management Association, 1968.

Szabados, Joseph. "Hungary's NEM: Promises and Pitfalls." East Europe 17 (April 1968): 25-32.

Taborsky, Edward. "Czechoslovakia's Economic Reform: Balance Sheet of the First Year." East Europe 17 (April 1968): 19-24.

Tamedly, Elisabeth L. Socialism and International Economic Order. Caldwell, Idaho: Caxton Printers, 1969.

"Test aus Moskau." Der Spiegel 10 (March 1, 1976): 105.

Thalheim, Karl C. "The Development of the East German Economy in the Framework of the Soviet Bloc." In Eastern Europe in Transition, edited by Kurt London, pp. 145-71. Baltimore: Johns Hopkins Press, 1966.

"The Advantages of An Investment Bank." East Europe 19 (November 1970): 42-43.

"The Comecon Charter." In Comecon: Integration Problems of the Planned Economies, edited by Michael Kaser, pp. 235-46. New York: Oxford University Press, 1967.

"The Debt That Overhangs East-West Dealings." Business Week, May 3, 1976, pp. 118-19.

"The Investment Bank." East Europe 19 (November 1970): 45-46.

"Trade With Socialist Nations Maintains Favorable Balance." Commerce Today 5 (August 4, 1975): 23.

Tyler, Geoffrey, and Hubert Neiss. "Problems and Prospects in East-West Trade." Finance and Development 10 (September 1973): 24-26.

"U.K. Loan to Comecon." East Europe 21 (May 1972): 31.

Ulc, Otto. "Czechoslovakia: The Great Leap Backward." In The Politics of Modernization in Eastern Europe, edited by Charles Gati, pp. 89-116. New York: Praeger, 1974.

United States Department of Commerce. "Czechoslovakia." Foreign Economic Trends ET 74-029 (April 1974).

____. "Czechoslovakia." Foreign Economic Trends FET 75-053 (June 1975).

____. "Doing Business With Czechoslovakia." Overseas Business Reports OBR 74-15 (June 1974).

____. "Hungary." Foreign Economic Trends FET 74-072 (August 1974).

____. "Hungary." Foreign Economic Trends FET 75-103 (August 1975).

____. "Poland." Foreign Economic Trends ET 74-017 (April 1974).

____. "Romania." Foreign Economic Trends ET 74-093 (September 1974).

____. "Trade of the United States With Socialist Countries in Eastern Europe and Asia, 1971-73." Overseas Business Reports OBR 74-24 (June 1974).

____. "Trading and Investing in Romania." Overseas Business Reports OBR 73-36 (August 1973).

____. "Trading in Hungary." Overseas Business Reports OBR 74-32 (July 1974).

____. "Trading in Poland." Overseas Business Reports OBR 73-50 (October 1973).

____. "World Trade Outlook for Eastern Europe, Union of Soviet Socialist Republics and People's Republic of China." Overseas Business Reports OBR 74-13 (May 1974).

____. "World Trade Outlook For Eastern Europe, Union of Soviet Socialist Republics and People's Republic of China." Overseas Business Reports OBR 75-19 (March 1975).

"U.S. Industry, Government Officials, Soviet Spokesman Call For Trade Continuity." Commerce Today 5 (March 3, 1975): 20.

Venema, Maynard P. "The Rumanian Refinery Project—The Negotiation, Structure, and Finance of a Major American Corporate Venture in Eastern Europe." In Financing East-West Business Transactions, edited by American Management Association, pp. 32-37. New York: American Management Association, 1968.

Wasowski, Stanislaw. "East-West Trade and the Pattern of World Trade." In East-West Trade and the Technology Gap: A Political and Economic Appraisal, edited by Stanislaw Wasowski, pp. 171-93. New York: Praeger, 1970.

Wesolowski, J. "Monetary and Financial Relations." In The Market of Socialist Economic Integration, edited by T. Kiss, pp. 203-11. Budapest: Akademiai Kiado, 1973.

Wilcsek, J. "Interrelations Between the National Economic Management Systems and the Socialist International Market Mechanism." In The Market of Socialist Economic Integration, edited by T. Kiss, pp. 99-107. Budapest: Akademiai Kiado, 1973.

Wilczynski, J. Profit, Risk and Incentives Under Socialist Economic Planning. London: Macmillan Press, 1973.

____. Socialist Economic Development and Reforms. New York: Praeger, 1972.

____. The Economics of Socialism. London: Allen and Unwin, 1970.

Wolf, Thomas A. "East-West Trade Credit Policy: A Comparative Analysis." In U.S. Financing of East-West Trade, edited by Paul Marer, pp. 149-199. Bloomington: International Development Research Center, 1975.

____. U.S. East-West Trade Policy. Lexington, Massachussetts: Heath, 1973.

Zemelka, Stanley. "The Problem of Specialization in Comecon." East Europe 18 (May 1969): 9-14.

Zielinski, Janusz G. Economic Reforms in Polish Industry. London: Oxford University Press, 1973.

____. On The Theory of Socialist Planning. London: Oxford University Press, 1968.

Zsoldos, Laszlo. Economic Integration of Hungary Into the Soviet Bloc: Foreign Trade Experience. Columbus, Ohio: Ohio State University, 1963.

Zurawicki, Leon. "The Cooperation of the Socialist State with the MNCs." Columbia Journal of World Business 10 (Spring 1975): 109-15.

INDEX

ABOUT THE AUTHOR

JOHN S. GARLAND is a graduate student of International Business at the University of Indiana in Bloomington. He has taught foreign languages in Kansas, Illinois, and Austria. He holds a B. S. and an M. S. in Education from the University of Kansas, where he majored in German Literature. He received his M.B.A. from Wichita State University in the Spring of 1976.

RELATED TITLES
Published by
Praeger Special Studies

EAST-WEST BUSINESS TRANSACTIONS
edited by Robert Starr

ECONOMIC DEVELOPMENT IN THE SOVIET UNION AND EASTERN EUROPE: Vol. I. Reforms, Technology, and Income Distribution; Vol. II. Sectoral Analysis
edited by Zbigniew M. Fallenbuchl

FOREIGN TRADE AND U.S. POLICY: The Case for Free International Trade*
Leland B. Yeager and David G. Tuerck

THE INTERNATIONAL POLITICS OF EASTERN EUROPE*
edited by Charles Gati

MODERNIZATION IN ROMANIA SINCE WORLD WAR II
Trond Gilberg

THE MULTINATIONAL BUSINESSMAN AND FOREIGN POLICY: Entrepreneurial Politics in East-West Trade and Investment
Jeffrey M. Brookstone

MULTINATIONAL CORPORATIONS AND EAST EUROPEAN SOCIALIST ECONOMIES
Geza P. Lauter and Paul M. Dickie

PERSONAL AND SOCIAL CONSUMPTION IN EASTERN EUROPE: Poland, Czechoslovakia, Hungary, and East Germany
Bogdan Mieczkowski

THE POLITICAL ECONOMY OF EAST-WEST TRADE
Connie M. Friesen

*Also available in paperback as a PSS Student Edition.